RECIPES FOR BUSY PEOPLE WHO LOVE GOOD FOOD

With three little boys less than two years apart and a packed schedule as an online creator, Caroline Chambers often doesn't feel like cooking. Can you relate? When you just can't motivate yourself in the kitchen, this is the book you should reach for.

Inspired by Caro's wildly popular Substack newsletter of the same name, *What to Cook When You Don't Feel Like Cooking* is brimming with efficient recipes that take the guesswork out of dinner—in fact, each one is a complete meal: protein, veg, starch, done! The recipes are organized by the amount of time they take to cook, so whether you have 15 minutes to throw together **Peanutty Pork and Brussels** or a little bit longer to simmer **Turkey Bolognese with Sneaky Veggies,** dinnertime is totally doable. On top of that, Caro gives you more ways to choose, so you can search by protein (Chicken thighs waiting in the fridge? Make **White Chicken Chili.** Nothing but beans in the pantry? **Cannellini Caprese with Burrata** is it!) or mood (**Tomato Farrotto** is perfect for a cozy craving, and **Crunchy Honey Harissa Fish Tacos** are an excellent way to show off). Most importantly, these recipes include Caro's famously extensive swaps, riffs, tips, shortcuts, and more to be sure they work best for you, helping you save money, improvise, and even learn a thing or two. They don't compromise quality or flavor—and they deliver every time. With as few ingredients, steps, and, of course, dirty dishes as possible, dinner awaits!

WHAT TO COOK WHEN YOU DON'T FEEL LIKE COOKING

WHAT TO COOK
WHEN YOU DON'T FEEL LIKE COOKING

CAROLINE CHAMBERS

UNION
SQUARE
& CO.

NEW YORK

Photographs by
Eva Kolenko

TO MY BEASTS:
I DON'T ALWAYS
FEEL LIKE
COOKING, BUT I
ALWAYS WANT
TO EAT YOU UP

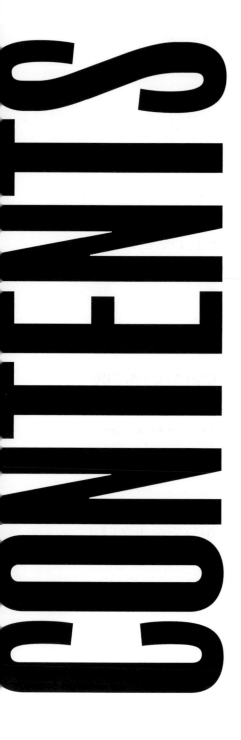

CONTENTS

45 MINUTES

1 HOUR

A LITTLE BIT LONGER

OBLIGATORY GREENS

OBLIGATORY SWEETS

HI! I'M CAROLINE.

My friends call me Caro— and you can, too.

If you've grabbed this book and flipped it open, then you and I have at least one thing in common: Sometimes, we don't feel like cooking.

I was raised in Winston-Salem, North Carolina, on the flavors of the South—smoky, sweet, tangy, and *fried* are in my blood. My mom is a wonderful cook who can turn a seemingly empty pantry into a gorgeous meal in no time. (She will, however, dirty up every single dish in the entire house in the process). She and my dad both worked and had to juggle three busy kids' school and activity schedules—but family dinner was always a priority.

My mom is the queen of time-saving tricks and hacks, and I've been learning how to turn chaos into a gorgeous meal since I was on her hip, but it wasn't until I was in my early twenties that I started my official food career in Coronado, California, where my husband, George, was stationed as a Navy SEAL.

Despite having very little professional kitchen experience, I opened a catering company within a few weeks of moving to Coronado. I was eager to share my passion for food with others, and being in the back of a restaurant on a prep line didn't feel like the way to do that. I wanted to be in the action, talking with my clients, telling them where their food—and the inspiration behind my recipes—had come from.

When I had larger events, I'd hire SEAL wives and neighbors to come schlep chafing dishes all across San Diego. It was a *grind*—catering is not for the faint of heart, but I learned a lot about portioning food properly, efficiency in the kitchen, and, most important, I learned what kinds of foods make people feel joy. The flavors that make them do the happy wiggles. The recipes they would come back into the kitchen begging for.

Life next took us to the Bay Area, where George attended Stanford Business School and I transitioned from catering to recipe development. I worked in the test kitchen at The Culinary Edge (TCE) in San Francisco, creating recipes and menus for national restaurant brands such as Panera Bread, Quiznos, and McAlister's. I got schooled in the importance of writing perfectly clear, precise recipes—recipes that could be followed by a teenager with zero kitchen experience who just got hired yesterday to work the line at a fast-food chain.

While working at TCE, I started doing freelance recipe development as a side hustle as well: I spent my nights and weekends developing recipes for brands and publications such as Mark West Wine, Kim Crawford Wine, Corona Beer, Boursin cheese, and many more. My side hustle quickly overtook my main hustle, so I left TCE to work as a full-time freelance recipe developer.

After George graduated from Stanford, we moved to Carmel-by-the-Sea, where he began his next endeavor in the medical research space. I published my first cookbook, *Just Married*, in 2018, and we had our first son, Mattis, two months later.

I continued to work as a freelance recipe developer, creating recipes for brands and publications. When the global pandemic began in March 2020, my freelance work went away, suddenly and completely—brands didn't know how to talk about food in the face of a global pandemic. But creators did! Suddenly everyone was forced to cook at home (shout-out to the banana bread and sourdough mania of 2020), and they needed recipes. I knew it was my opportunity to start publishing recipes from *me*—not recipes that I developed because a brand needed something for their marketing materials. I'd been wanting to do this for years, but I'd been too busy with my freelance work.

I started cranking out easy, straightforward recipes that lockdown-weary folks could cook using whatever they had in their pantries. I provided a substitution for every single ingredient to ensure that even if your store was out of something or you didn't want to take another trip to the supermarket, you could still make the recipe. I posted it all on my Instagram and quickly grew a community of like-minded folks who love eating good food but don't have the time or patience to cook it.

Swaps and riffs became my *thing.* I loved showing people that even if you don't have halibut, you can make the same recipe using chicken! No basil? Any soft herb will do! No cashews? Use whatever nut or seed is handy!

I had my second baby boy, Calum, in September 2020, and then in December, I launched *What to Cook When You Don't Feel Like Cooking* as a subscription-based newsletter on Substack. I was fatigued, to be sure, but I knew the entire world had extreme cooking fatigue, too. To get dinner on the table every night, I found myself coming up with kitchen hacks and shortcuts that were wildly un-*cheffy*—but they worked, and they yielded delicious results with far less effort than your typical recipe. They were the types of tricks and hacks my mom had taught me, and I wanted everyone to have access to them.

I had no idea if *What to Cook* would succeed. Would people be willing to pay for a subscription to my recipes when there was so much free content already on the internet? *Dang*, turned out they sure would. My people showed up. *What to Cook* shot to the top of the Substack leaderboard overnight.

Since then, my family has grown with the addition of the littlest brother, Cashel, and my newsletter has continued to grow, too, as emails are forwarded, gorgeous pics are shared on Instagram, recipes are cooked up for dinner parties and family reunions, and links to favorite recipes are shared on group chats.

Maybe that's how you found me, or maybe you were one of my original one thousand subscribers. Or maybe you just liked the title (isn't it good?) and grabbed this book off the shelf.

Whoever you are and however you arrived, I'm glad you're here, and I'm excited to cook with you in these pages.

Hi! I'm Caroline. **11**

ABOUT THIS BOOK

The ethos of *What to Cook* is to prepare delicious food with as little effort as possible. What has made my newsletter so popular is exactly what you'll find in this book.

When I don't feel like cooking, time is usually the biggest roadblock. With that in mind, I've organized this book into big chapters based on how long the recipes take to make. That way, you can look at the clock or glance at your calendar for the week, assess how much time you'll have in the kitchen, and choose accordingly. That's usually where I start!

Having friends over for dinner, but have zero time to cook and plan a feast that will impress them? The Roasted Salmon & Asparagus with Dilly Sauce (page 40) will be ready in 15 minutes.

Want to cook a really nice meal for you and your partner, but you're exhausted after a long day at the office? You can have Lemony Garlic Butter Shrimp Orzo (page 91) on the table in 30 minutes—it's simple to prepare and looks absolutely beautiful.

Stay-at-home mom with exactly one time block during which you can put dinner together? You can throw together the Sriracha Shrimp Sushi Bowls (page 156) while you feed the kids lunch. Or maybe you work from home and have time throughout the day to peel, chop, and prepare a meal in sections. Sheet Pan Chicken Poblano Fajitas (page 191) are perfect for you—ready in 1 hour with just one pan to clean at the end! I've also included a shorter chapter of lengthier recipes for when you have the luxury of a bit more time.

If time is not the determining factor of your life, first, please tell me the magic of your ways. But then, rest assured that I've also created multiple indexes to help you browse in different ways. The next defining factor for me is either *What do I have on hand?* or *What do I feel like eating?* So you can search by protein type. And then I ask myself, *What's the vibe?* If you're having friends over this weekend, look up a "What to Cook When You Want to Show Off" recipe (page 262). If you just got back from pounding pasta in Italy for two weeks and need a little reset, check the "What to Cook When You're Feeling Especially Healthy" section (page 260).

Once you find your recipe, what can you expect? Perhaps the most special part of this cookbook is that every single recipe is a complete meal. There's no sides chapter, there are no sneaky subrecipes that will take you an extra hour to cook. (There are, however, obligatory greens and obligatory sweets for when you just need a little something extra!) My goal is to take the guesswork out of mealtime for you—everything you need for dinner is right there on the page.

In that spirit, just like in my newsletter (and even more so here), I've also provided key notes and swap ideas for every recipe. They're broken down into the following categories:

TIP
General cooking tips pertinent to the individual recipe.

SLOW
I know a lot of people who don't feel like cooking often turn to their slow cookers for help. Throw a bunch of things in a pot, turn a dial, and come back to dinner a few hours later? Yes, that works. I've provided tips on how to make these recipes in a slow cooker wherever possible.

SHORTCUT
These are some time-saving tips for shaving minutes off your cook time without sacrificing flavor. I use them all the time.

LEARN
Tips that will make you a better cook. Sometimes these just call out something you'll do in that recipe to explain *why* you're doing it that way. "Teach a man to fish," if you will. These tips elaborate on a technique or break down a process.

RIFF
Once you know how to cook one recipe, you actually know how to cook ten recipes! All you have to do is swap in a different protein, veggie, or sauce, and *bam!*—you have a completely new meal. In Riffs, I'll give you a few ideas for how to riff on that recipe to transform it into a different dish.

SWAP
I've said it before and I'll say it again: I always encourage swapping in whatever proteins, veggies, grains, etc., you already have on hand in favor of shopping for new ingredients! These notes will give you some ideas to get your culinary imagination going, but you have my full permission to use whatever works for you. Check out page 20 for some starter ideas!

BULK IT UP
While every recipe in this cookbook is a complete meal, you might find some instances in which you want the meal to feed more people, or hungrier people, or you just want to provide more options. These tips will give you ideas on what will pair perfectly with the recipe.

IF YOU CAN ONLY TAKE AWAY ONE THING FROM THIS BOOK, IT'S THIS: <u>DO YOUR THING!</u> COOKING DOES NOT HAVE TO BE STRESSFUL. MAYBE YOU'LL NEVER LOVE IT, BUT MAN, DON'T LET IT STRESS YOU OUT. MISSING AN INGREDIENT? SWAP IN SOMETHING ELSE, OR OMIT IT. BURNED THE ONIONS? SCRAPE OUT AS MANY OF THE CHARRED ONES AS YOU CAN, THEN CARRY ON. MEAT TAKING LONGER TO COOK THAN THE RECIPE SAYS? POUR YOURSELF A GLASS OF WINE AND CHILL OUT WHILE YOU WAIT. SOME NIGHTS IT WILL BE EASIEST TO USE THESE RECIPES AS AN EXACT GUIDE, OTHER NIGHTS IT WILL BE BEST TO USE THEM AS A LOOSE TEMPLATE TO USE UP WHATEVER YOU HAVE IN THE FRIDGE. DO. YOUR. THING!

How to Make Yourself Cook Even When You Really, Really Don't Feel Like It

1. Order groceries online while you watch your nightly TV show, or while you're in the bath, or while you're waiting for your kid to finish their piano lesson.

2. Invite a friend (or another family!) over for dinner—they bring a side, you make the entree, you all get to socialize. Win, win, win.

3. Prep throughout the day—chop the herbs during a free moment after breakfast, make the dressing while you're on a conference call on mute, let your kiddo help peel the carrots as an activity.

4. Pop in your earbuds and put on a podcast or a book you can get lost in (I am partial to smutty romance), or call your mom.

5. Reach your arm *deep* into the back of your pantry. Grab a bag/canister/jar that you haven't even seen in a few months. Use the index (page 264) to find a recipe to use that ingredient, or even just google "recipes using [fill in the blank]." Sometimes inspiration is lurking in a dark corner behind the slivered almonds!

6. Similarly, locate a protein in your freezer or fridge. Flip to the list on page 258 and pick your favorite recipe.

7. Have your partner/kid/parent/roommate/babysitter come into the kitchen every few minutes while you're cooking to clean all the dirty dishes. My husband is a pro at this—he cleans as I cook, so by the time dinner's over, all we have to do is load our plates into the dishwasher.

8. Pick up a really good loaf of bread to serve with dinner—from that cool new bakery in town—and enjoy it with plenty of butter and salt while you cook. Just don't fill up so much that you don't have an appetite for the delicious meal you cooked!

9. If cooking feels like a waste of time to you, get in some exercise while you do it. Bring weights into the kitchen and do bicep curls while you wait for water to boil. Squats while you broil. Calf raises while you sauté. And so on.

10. Call your best friend and ask them what the most delicious thing they've cooked lately was. Then cook it immediately.

11. Go to the farmers' market. It's fun! Buy one new vegetable. If it's a hard vegetable, swap it in for another hard vegetable in a recipe you know you love. If it's a soft vegetable, same. Cooking new things is not as difficult as it seems!

12. Keep your favorite quick tricks on hand at all times: Trader Joe's frozen dumplings, Costco pesto, Lotus Foods ramen noodles, and Rao's jarred marinara are my lifelines.

13. Lean into grocery store convenience. Sliced mushrooms, frozen diced onions, frozen rice, frozen minced garlic and ginger cubes, prechopped sweet potatoes—these are all your friends, and they can be your sous chefs, too.

14. Grab the nonstick skillet. A good nonstick will simply make your life easier—your food won't stick and frustrate you, and cleanup will be a breeze. (There's a caveat to this one: When you want good browning or a nice crusty sear, pull out the stainless steel or cast iron.)

15. Swap, don't shop. If you have a freezer full of pork tenderloin, use it in place of boneless chicken. If you're out of honey, use sugar or maple syrup. You'll find a whole list of smart substitutions on page 20, but you should also trust your gut—proteins and sweet, salty, acidic, and fatty flavors can be swapped around based on what you have in the pantry.

16. Choose a recipe from the 15-ish Minutes chapter. You. Can. Do. This.

17. Keep a stack of nice thick compostable paper plates in the pantry at all times. Fewer dishes = less cooking dread.

18. Keep a large, pretty wooden cutting board on your counter at all times (I love my 20 × 15-inch Boos Block). Wipe it down with a sponge after using it. Not having to pull out a cutting board, wash it, and put it away every single time I chop something makes me dread the chopping process that much less.

19. Remember that with the right mindset, cooking can be fun! Calming! Inspiring! Take a deep breath and reframe dinnertime. Stressful day? Use cooking dinner to take your mind off the stress and unwind. Cuckoo kids? Use cooking as an excuse to make your spouse entertain the kids while you cook. You got this.

Equip Yourself

It can be incredibly frustrating to get halfway through a recipe only to realize you don't own all the tools necessary to get across the finish line. These are the most-used tools in my kitchen, and the *only* tools used in the recipes in this book. Once you've loaded up your kitchen with this gear, you're golden.

MIXING BOWLS

SILICONE SPATULA

12-INCH CAST-IRON SKILLET

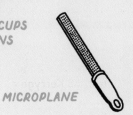

MEASURING CUPS AND SPOONS

CHEF'S KNIFE

MICROPLANE

WHISK

LIQUID MEASURING CUP

COLANDER

A LARGE, PRETTY (BECAUSE IT SHOULD SIT ON YOUR COUNTERTOP AT ALL TIMES) WOODEN CUTTING BOARD

LONG AND SHORT TONGS WITH SILICONE TIPS

TWO RIMMED 18 X 13-INCH BAKING SHEETS (*IF YOUR OVEN CAN FIT A FULL 26 X 18-INCH PAN, GET ONE OF THOSE TOO!*)

SILICONE FISH SPATULA

LARGE STOCKPOT

13 X 9-INCH BAKING DISH

BOX GRATER

KITCHEN SHEARS

INSTANT-READ THERMOMETER

WOODEN SPOON

10- AND 12-INCH NONSTICK SKILLETS. I ALSO LOVE MY 14-INCH SKILLET FOR COOKING LARGER QUANTITIES.

3-QUART SAUCEPAN WITH A LID

Ingredients to Keep on Hand

These are the ingredients I always have in my kitchen. If you keep them stocked in yours, too, you will never be far from cooking most of the recipes in these pages.

BUTTER. I like Challenge for unsalted and Kerrygold for salted.

DIAMOND CRYSTAL KOSHER SALT is the only brand I use. If you use another brand, your recipes will taste different.

FLAKY SEA SALT, such as Maldon or Jacobsen, is a large, pretty salt. I use it to finish dishes and give them a bit of salty sparkle.

EXTRA-VIRGIN OLIVE OIL. I cook almost exclusively with extra-virgin olive oil—, it's SO GOOD FOR YOU, and it tastes great.

NEUTRAL OIL can be avocado (my preference), grapeseed, vegetable, canola, or sunflower seed.

SESAME OIL tastes great in Asian cooking, or when I want to add a savory, nutty boost to any dish.

ACIDIC THINGS, like lemons, limes, apple cider vinegar, balsamic vinegar . . .

GRAINS. I keep frozen, microwaveable rice in the freezer for busy nights, as well as pretty much every type of rice—brown, jasmine, Arborio, sushi—in the pantry. Farro and quinoa are great to have on hand.

PASTA. Ramen noodles, spaghetti, and a few fun short noodle shapes.

STOCK is just unseasoned broth, and you can always use the two interchangeably, but the recipes in this book always call for stock, which gives you control over how much salt is in your dish—and I always buy low-sodium stock for the most control. I am also a huge fan of Better Than Bouillon, a stock concentrate that you mix into water. I always have the chicken, veggie, and beef flavors in my fridge. And I don't just use it in recipes that call for stock! I also stir a little spoonful into a dish that needs a punch of savory flavor, like a soup, a stir-fry, or a pasta sauce.

DAIRY. Whole milk, Greek yogurt, feta, Parm, and sharp cheddar can take you far. If you're dairy-free, you can find great alternatives for all of these. Buying pregrated fresh cheese is fine, but avoid the super cheap stuff, as it contains anti-caking agents that will mess with your recipe; I always check the ingredients.

SAUCES like marinara, pesto, harissa, nut butter, and salsa can make almost anything taste good.

HOT-SAUCE-Y THINGS like Mexican hot sauce, sriracha, and gochujang are a must.

ROASTY VEGETABLES, like potatoes, carrots, fennel, cauliflower.

QUICK-COOKING VEGETABLES, like zucchini, frozen corn, peas, bell peppers.

FRUIT. I think buying and eating seasonal fruit is one of life's simplest, greatest pleasures. Strawberries and peaches in the heart of summer, figs in the early days of fall, apples in the fall, citrus and pears in the winter, and apricots as winter turns to spring.

NUTS AND SEEDS make the best snack and crunchy garnish. I usually buy my nuts roasted and salted.

MEAT. I keep boneless, skinless chicken breasts and thighs, peeled and deveined large shrimp, and a few pounds of ground meat in the freezer at all times. They thaw quickly when submerged in room-temp water, so they're perfect for the "oops, I forgot to thaw the meat!" scramble. And I always have a pound of deli-sliced turkey or ham in the fridge for sandwiches or throwing into salads.

FRESH HERBS can be a massive, low-cost game changer (a bunch of herbs is typically about $2). I always have a bunch of flat-leaf parsley and cilantro in the fridge (keep them wrapped in a slightly damp paper towel in a zip-top bag) or growing in the garden. I use basil like a madwoman when it's in season in the summer. I also use thyme, rosemary, and mint regularly.

Let's Talk About Seasoning

Have you ever cooked something—maybe a recipe you were really excited about, maybe something you made up on the fly—and had really high expectations, but then when you took that first bite . . . meh. Boring.

It's the worst feeling in the world, and it is preventable. You must season as you go, every step of the way, but especially when you get to the end. Before you transfer any food onto plates or into bowls, you have to taste it!

Does it lack taste in general? Add salt. **Salt makes food taste more like itself**. It punches up the natural flavors.

Does it taste too rich, or just kind of flat? Add acid (citrus or vinegar).

Too boring? Maybe it needs some heat (red pepper flakes or hot sauce).

Every vegetable, every cut of meat, and, most important, every palate is different, so you must adjust it to suit your taste buds and the exact food that you are cooking. And then don't be offended if someone you're serving it to seasons it further to suit *their* palate.

And by the way, let's put a stop to something right here and now.

Are you seasoning your food using a freakin' saltshaker? Today's the day we put an end to that.

Take your salt (preferably Diamond Crystal kosher salt), pour it into a bowl, and keep it by the stove at all times. I almost *never* measure salt when I'm cooking—I pinch it with my fingers, add it to my food, taste, and repeat until it tastes perfect. I provide lots of precise salt measurements in this book, just in case you need them, but I encourage you to ignore them and measure with your fingers, tasting and adding more as you go. The more you do this, the easier and more intuitive seasoning will become.

Salt makes food taste food-ier. More like itself. It should not make it taste *salty*. Seasoning with salt is arguably the most important part of cooking, and practice makes perfect. Salt, taste, repeat!

OH, AND PS.

You do not always have to use pepper. The history of why Americans use so much black pepper in our cooking is fascinating, and it boils down to this: good marketing. Pepper is not an ingredient that needs to be in every single thing that you cook. (Salt, however, is! In case that wasn't clear.)

How to Swap It

PROTEINS

You can swap proteins liberally! As a general rule, if it has a bone in it, it'll take longer to cook, and the less fatty it is, the quicker it'll cook. Use your instant-read thermometer and don't stray too far from the oven during the last 5 to 10 minutes of cooking. Keep a close eye to ensure the protein doesn't overcook. You can swap in any ground meat for any ground meat following the same rules.

CARBY THINGS

With one-pot pastas, short noodles (rotini, penne, rigatoni) and long noodles (spaghetti, linguine, bucatini) can be subbed for each other. If it's not a one-pot sitch, you can pretty much swap any noodle.

TANGY

An acidic, tangy, sour element is sometimes just what a dish needs to bring it to life. A squeeze of lime juice over a taco, a splash of vinegar into a veggie sauté. Clear-ish vinegars like apple cider or red wine vinegar can be used interchangeably. Balsamic is typically (though not always) sweeter, so if you're using a clear vinegar in place of balsamic, consider adding a bit of sweetness (honey or sugar) as well. Lemon and lime juice are great tangy additions, as are some cheeses, like feta, goat cheese, or an extra-sharp cheddar. Even breads can sometimes bring the acidic hit you need—for instance, a sourdough crouton on a salad.

COOKING FAT

We are using extra-virgin olive oil as our cooking fat in most of the recipes in this book because it has incredible health benefits, it adds rich flavor, and the myth that it has a low smoke point has been debunked. Many brands, including Kosterina and Graza, now make "cooking" extra-virgin olive oils and "just for drizzling" extra-virgin olive oils that are sold at different price points. If EVOO is ever too expensive when I'm shopping, I grab plain olive oil instead, which is a more refined product with fewer, but still plenty of, health benefits.

Any time a rich, olive-y flavor is not wanted, I call for neutral oil (avocado is my go-to). It's called neutral oil because its flavor is, well, neutral.

Don't cook with butter over high heat (it'll burn!), but it is great for low-heat cooking when you want to add richness.

Coconut oil and sesame oil are other favorite oils, but they do add a specific flavor, so only use them when that's what you're after.

SALT

Believe it or not, all salts are not created equal. As I mentioned, my gold standard salt is Diamond Crystal. If you're swapping in table salt, use 50 percent less (so if the recipe calls for 1 teaspoon kosher, use ½ teaspoon table salt).

For finishing, in place of flaky sea salt, you can try soy sauce, fish sauce, capers, bacon, or Parmesan cheese.

FATS

When you take a bite of a dish, if it just tastes too light and you find yourself craving a fatty element, you have a lot of options. Cheese is most often *my* solution—a crumble of feta over a salad, a swipe of ricotta onto a toast, or a sprinkle of cheddar in scrambled eggs might transform your dish. More neutral-tasting cheeses (provolone, cheddar, even American) can be swapped around easily, but a cheese like feta or goat cheese will also bring a tangy element, so don't add as much.

Creamy white things like mayo and yogurt and sour cream can, for the most part, swap nicely for each other.

Maybe you're dairy-free— you can try subbing in a salty, crunchy, fatty nut, or a briny olive. Adding a nut butter to a sauce or salad dressing will help thicken it up and might balance it out if you want something less acidic.

Sometimes if I make a big salad and it's feeling boring, all it needs is a bit more extra-virgin olive oil and salt, and then it's perfect!

SWEET

When swapping in a sweet element, always start with less, then add more if you need it. Honey, white sugar, brown sugar, maple syrup—feel free to swap these around. Will the flavor be the same? Not quite! But you'll still be achieving a sweet note, which is the end goal.

SPICY

Sriracha, Cholula, sambal oelek, gochujang, chili crisp—I love them all! Each has a distinct flavor profile, but you can certainly swap one for another, again, starting with a just a little and adding more as desired. When in doubt, always keep red pepper flakes on hand to add heat to dishes. Freshly ground black pepper is also a good option—lots of it packs quite a punch!

TENDER GREENS

These are greens that require very little work to be delicious. Think salad greens we don't need to cook (but can!): romaine, arugula, spinach, butter lettuce, Little Gem, mixed greens, microgreens, watercress . . . basically anything that comes in a plastic bag or a clamshell in the salad-y section of the refrigerated aisle at the grocery store. I'm also going to put kale and cabbage in this category— once you strip out the tough stem, chop, and massage it with a little salt, it can masquerade as a tender green.

HEARTY GREENS

These greens require a little more coaxing to get them to taste delicious. They're delicious sautéed or braised, perhaps in a stew. Kale and cabbage can also fall into this category, as do bok choy, chard, collards, and beet greens.

HARD VEGGIES

Hard, dense vegetables are interchangeable. Sure, I might roast a sweet potato for less time than a russet potato, but is the end result going to be delicious? Yes, yes it is. Hard veggies that you can swap around include: any kind of potato, kohlrabi (a dark horse!), rutabaga, parsnips, carrots, cauliflower, onions, winter squashes, pumpkin, beets, celery root, turnips, romanesco, carrots.

SOFT VEGGIES

Soft, tender veggies are also widely interchangeable! Corn, zucchini, summer squash, eggplant, broccoli, okra, bell peppers. Swap them around!

15-ISH MINUTES

BUTTER-BASTED CAST-IRON RIB EYES
& Swiss Chard with Garlicky Crunchies

2 slices crusty bread (fresh or day-old), or ½ cup panko breadcrumbs

4 tablespoons (½ stick) unsalted butter

½ teaspoon garlic powder

Kosher salt and freshly ground black pepper

2 large (about 14-ounce) rib eye steaks

Extra-virgin olive oil

6 garlic cloves

2 bunches Swiss chard

4 rosemary sprigs

1 tablespoon apple cider vinegar (or any vinegar or lemon juice)

LEARN
If you add a steak to a skillet that's warm, not sizzlin' hot, you'll wind up with a soft, grayish exterior instead of the golden brown crust we're going for.

SHORTCUT
Grab store-bought croutons, crush them up, and use those instead of making the garlicky crunchies!

SERVES 4

George and I love this meal on a lazy Sunday night—it feels decadent and cozy but requires very little effort. We put the kids to bed as early as possible, then get into the kitchen and cook together. At the end, we're rewarded with a succulent, buttery steak, a tangle of tangy wilted greens, and a garlicky crunch to provide the perfect texture contrast in every bite.

1. Chop the **bread** into teeny pieces to get ½ to ¾ cup breadcrumbs. Melt **2 tablespoons of the butter** in a cast-iron skillet over medium heat. Add the breadcrumbs, **garlic powder**, **½ teaspoon salt**, and **¼ teaspoon pepper** and cook, stirring often, until deeply golden brown, 4 to 5 minutes. Transfer the breadcrumbs to a plate. Wipe out the skillet, then return it to medium-high heat.

2. Meanwhile, season the **rib eyes** with salt and pepper, roughly 1 teaspoon of salt per pound of meat. Rub a thin layer of **olive oil** all over the steaks.

3. When you flick a drop of water into the pan and it dances around, it's hot enough. Add the steaks. Cook until a golden brown crust appears on the bottom, 5 to 6 minutes.

4. While they're cooking, use the side of your knife to smash **4 garlic cloves**. Thinly slice the other **2 garlic cloves**. Trim off the very ends of the stalks from the **Swiss chard**, then thinly slice the stalks and roughly chop the leaves.

5. Flip the steaks and add the smashed garlic cloves, the **rosemary sprigs**, and the remaining **2 tablespoons butter** to the skillet. When the butter has melted, carefully tilt the skillet toward you and use a large spoon to scoop up the butter and pour it over the steaks. Continue cooking like this until the second side is golden brown, about 4 minutes for medium-rare or 5 minutes for medium. (An instant-read thermometer should register 135°F for medium-rare or 145°F for medium.) Transfer the steaks to a plate and pour the melted butter, rosemary, and garlic over them.

6. Return the skillet to medium-high heat. Add **1 tablespoon oil** to the skillet, then add the 2 sliced garlic cloves and cook, stirring, until fragrant, about 30 seconds. Add half the chard and cook, stirring often, until the chard wilts enough to fit more into the skillet. Add the remaining chard, the **vinegar**, and **½ teaspoon salt**. Cook until the chard is wilted and tender, 5 to 6 minutes. Taste and add more salt as needed.

7. Cut the steak into ¼-inch-thick slices and divide among four plates. Use tongs to serve the chard, squeezing out any excess moisture before adding it to the plates. Top everything with the garlicky crunchies and dig in.

I PROMISE YOU CAN COOK MUSSELS

4 ounces chopped pancetta
4 garlic cloves
1 bunch chives
4 pounds mussels, scrubbed and debearded (see Learn)
½ cup dry white wine (I like sauvignon blanc)
½ cup crème fraîche or heavy cream
Absolutely any really good bread, sliced
Unsalted butter

LEARN
Ideally, you'll buy your mussels scrubbed and debearded (if you buy them from a good fish market, ask them to do this!), but if not, place the mussels in a bowl and cover with cold water for several minutes. This will make them spit out any grit. Then grab each mussel in one hand with a kitchen towel to keep it from slipping, and with another kitchen towel, clean it off. If you see a little hairy "beard" poking out of the shell, grab it with the kitchen towel and yank it out.

RIFF
Try coconut curry mussels: Ditch the pancetta, stir in 2 tablespoons curry paste, and use coconut cream instead of crème fraîche. Or just swap in clams!

SERVES 4

There's a restaurant in New York City called Flex Mussels that my friends and I used to frequent when I lived there in my twenties. It's the coziest little spot, and the entire menu is—you guessed it—different variations of mussels. We'd get a couple different bowls of mussels, a ton of bread for dunking, and a crisp bottle of Sancerre and share everything. Now I love cooking mussels at home—it's truly SO EASY, whether it's a dinner party or a simple weeknight meal at home, and they make for such a fun vibe, with everyone opening the mussels and ripping off bread to dunk into the sauce. This is my all-time favorite super-simple mussels recipe, and in the Riffs I've also included a curry version that I love, too.

1. Heat the broiler to high.

2. Place the **pancetta** in a large, deep pot and cook over medium heat, stirring every minute or so, until crisp, 5 to 7 minutes.

3. Meanwhile, mince the **garlic** and finely chop the **chives** (I like to use kitchen scissors for this). Measure and set aside 2 tablespoons of the chives. Add the remaining chives and all the garlic to the crispy pancetta in the pot and cook, stirring frequently, until the garlic is fragrant, another minute. Add the **mussels** and **wine** to the pot, cover, and increase the heat to medium-high. Cook for 3 minutes, stir, then cover again and cook until most of the mussels have opened, another 5 to 6 minutes. Discard any mussels that haven't opened.

4. Stir the **crème fraîche** into the broth. Sprinkle the reserved chives over the top.

5. Meanwhile, place the **bread** on a baking sheet and add a little pat of **butter** to each slice. Broil for 1 to 3 minutes, until the bread is golden brown and the butter has melted. *Do not walk away from the oven! Butter burns quickly!*

6. Ladle the mussels and broth into four bowls and serve with the toasty, buttery bread alongside for sopping up the deliciousness.

GARLICKY GRAINS
with Asparagus & Sausage

1 bunch asparagus

1 pound cooked Italian chicken sausage or kielbasa

6 garlic cloves

½ cup fresh parsley leaves and tender stems

2 tablespoons extra-virgin olive oil

Kosher salt

2 cups cooked grains—barley, farro, brown rice, rice, or quinoa (whatever's on hand!)

2 tablespoons balsamic vinegar, plus more as needed

¾ teaspoon dried oregano

¾ teaspoon garlic powder

¼ teaspoon red pepper flakes

2 ounces goat, Parmesan, or feta cheese

SWAP
Use pork or turkey sausage in place of the chicken sausage—just cook it by itself in the skillet first, then add the asparagus and continue with the recipe. Green beans, broccoli, or thinly sliced bell peppers work great in place of asparagus. Cook times will vary—just get it crisp-tender!

SERVES 4

My kids absolutely *crush* chicken sausage—it's one of the reliable proteins (along with chicken fingers and hotdogs, duh) in their diet—so we always have a package in the fridge. If this meal seems a bit too complex for the picky eaters in your life, just cook the asparagus and sausage, pull out enough for the kids' plates, then continue with the recipe. That's how I often feed my family—we might not always eat the exact same meal, but I try to at least serve the kids disassembled versions of what we're eating.

1. Trim the **asparagus** and cut it into 1-inch pieces. Halve the **sausage** lengthwise, then slice it crosswise into half-moons. Thinly slice the **garlic**. Finely chop the **parsley**.

2. Warm the **olive oil** in a large skillet over medium-high heat. When it shimmers, add the asparagus, chicken sausage, and a **big pinch of salt** and cook, stirring occasionally, until the sausage is browned, 5 to 6 minutes. Add the garlic for the final 30 seconds.

3. Stir in the **cooked grains**, all but 2 tablespoons of the parsley, the **vinegar**, **oregano**, **garlic powder**, **red pepper flakes**, and **¼ teaspoon salt**. Stir until everything is combined well and warmed through, a minute or two.

4. Taste and adjust the seasonings as desired. (Some people [me] like a lot of salt and acid, so I always add more of those.)

5. Divide among four bowls. Crumble the **cheese** and sprinkle ½ ounce over each bowl. Finish with another sprinkle of parsley before you dig in.

CHEATER CHICKEN TINGA TOSTADAS

1 (14.5-ounce) can fire-roasted diced tomatoes
1 canned chipotle chile in adobo sauce
2 teaspoons low-sodium soy sauce
2 teaspoons apple cider vinegar
1 teaspoon dried oregano
1 teaspoon garlic powder
Kosher salt
1 rotisserie chicken
1 (16-ounce) can refried beans
8 tostadas
Toppings (optional): shredded iceberg lettuce, sour cream, cheese (Cotija or cheddar would be great here), thinly sliced red onion

SERVES 2

One of my former coworkers from the culinary consulting firm I worked at in San Francisco owns a Mexican restaurant in Richmond, Virginia, called En Su Boca, which means "in your mouth." (Double entendre: It's located in an old porn shop.) I asked him what I should cook for a dinner party one night, and he immediately printed out his restaurant's chicken tinga recipe for me and said, "Trust me on this one." I made it that night, and my guests lost their minds over it. Over the years, I've shortened it into a version I can pull off on a Tuesday night and still get the big, "in your mouth" flavor explosion that good, slow-simmered tinga delivers. Doctoring up an already perfectly cooked rotisserie chicken is one of my very best shortcuts.

1. Pour the **tomatoes** into a medium saucepan. Place over high heat. While it comes to a boil, stir in the **chipotle chile**, **soy sauce**, **vinegar**, **dried oregano**, **garlic powder**, and ¼ **teaspoon salt**. As soon as it comes to a boil, reduce the heat to medium-high. Using a fork, break up the chipotle chile into small bits.

2. Meanwhile, shred 3 cups of meat from the rotisserie **chicken**. Shred it finely—no big chunks of chicken, we want individual strands here—and discard the skin. Add the shredded chicken to the pot and cook, stirring frequently, until the chicken is warmed through and most of the liquid has evaporated, 3 to 4 minutes.

3. Spread a big spoonful of **refried beans** over each of the **tostadas**, then sprinkle with salt because they're typically a bit bland. Layer a big spoonful of the chicken tinga on top, then top however you please!

TIP I recommend making 1 tostada per person at a time, as they get soggy quickly. Try serving everything family-style so your guests can assemble their own tostadas right at the dinner table.

LEARN When you remove the pepper from the adobo sauce, remove the stem if there is one. For less spice, also remove the seeds.

RIFF The chicken tinga is also great in a bowl with rice, or as a taco, or in place of the turkey in Turkey Taco Salad (page 119).

SLOW If you want to forgo the rotisserie chicken and make this dish in a slow cooker, toss 1 1/2 pounds boneless, skinless chicken breasts or thighs and everything except the beans and tostadas into a slow cooker, cover, and cook on low for 6 hours. Shred and assemble as instructed.

other tricks you can perform with a

ROTISSERIE CHICKEN

HERBY CHICKEN SALAD
Shred 2 cups of chicken and stir in enough mayo to wet it, 1 tablespoon balsamic vinegar, 2 teaspoons Dijon mustard, 1/4 cup finely chopped dill, and salt and pepper to taste.

MANGO CHICKEN TACOS
Shred 3 cups of chicken, finely chop a mango, and stir them together with 1/3 cup salsa verde. Load the mixture into warmed-up tortillas with lots of cheese and/or avocado on top.

CHICKEN CURRY NOODLE SOUP
Add 1 1/2 cups of shredded chicken to the Coconut Curry Ramen & Veggie Noodle Soup (page 50).

COUSIN LEXIE'S TEX-MEX ENCHILADAS
Shred the entire chicken and stir it together with 1 (8-ounce) block softened cream cheese, 1 1/2 cups salsa verde, and 1 (4-ounce) jar green chiles. Roll it into tortillas, then smother it with more salsa verde (grab a second jar just in case you need it), and lots of shredded cheddar cheese. Cover with foil and bake at 350°F for 30 minutes, then remove the foil and bake for 15 minutes more. Make like Lexie and feed a crowd.

CHICKEN PARM SLIDERS
Use shredded chicken instead of making the chicken patty on page 140. Add sauce and cheese, then bake.

COUSIN KAT'S KALE CHICKEN SALAD
Stem 2 bunches of kale, chop the leaves, and massage with a big pinch of salt. Add 1/4 cup chopped mint leaves; half a shredded rotisserie chicken; 1 cup or so of cooked brown rice, orzo, or quinoa; 1/4 cup shaved Parmesan; 1/4 cup yellow raisins or chopped dates; and lots of lemon juice or extra-virgin olive oil. Do as Kat does and eat it all week; it keeps covered in the fridge for 3 to 4 days.

POULES FRITES
Carve a rotisserie chicken into pieces. Cook frozen french fries until super crispy. Grate a garlic clove into 1/2 cup mayo for a quickie garlic aioli.

GRILLED LEMON HARISSA CHICKEN & ZUCCHINI

2 pounds boneless, skinless chicken breasts and/or thighs

2 tablespoons plus 1 teaspoon harissa, plus more as needed

2 tablespoons extra-virgin olive oil

Kosher salt

1 lemon, plus more as needed

3 medium zucchini

¾ cup labneh, sour cream, or plain full-fat Greek yogurt

¼ cup soft herbs, such as dill, parsley, chives, basil, or a mix

TIP
No grill? Throw everything onto a parchment-lined rimmed baking sheet and roast at 425°F for 15 to 20 minutes, until the chicken breast reaches 160°F (it will continue cooking while it rests to reach a safe 165°F).

SERVES 4

I always have a jar of harissa on hand. This North African spice paste is made with dried chiles, garlic, citrus, and extra-virgin olive oil. I love using it as a quick marinade for meat, dolloping it into soup or scrambled eggs for a flavor boost, or stirring it into something creamy, such as sour cream or yogurt, to create a dipping sauce. The grill is my secret weapon for quick weeknight cooking—there's barely any cleanup afterward!

1. Heat an outdoor grill to medium-high (400° to 450°F).

2. In a large bowl, combine the **chicken**, **2 tablespoons of the harissa**, **1 tablespoon of the olive oil**, and **2 teaspoons salt**. Using a Microplane, grate in the zest of the **lemon**, then halve it and squeeze in the juice from one half (reserve the other half for the sauce). Toss to coat.

3. Halve the **zucchini** crosswise, then slice into ¼-inch-thick planks. Add the zucchini on top of the chicken (yes, it can touch the raw chicken), drizzle with the remaining **1 tablespoon oil**, and season with **¼ teaspoon salt**. Use your hands to coat the zucchini in oil and salt—it's fine if some of the harissa gets on the zucchini, but you don't want to totally toss the zucchini and chicken together.

4. Grill the chicken and zucchini for 5 to 7 minutes per side, or until the chicken registers 165°F on an instant-read thermometer and the zucchini is very, very tender—like, smushy! It's so good when it's a bit smushy. Transfer everything from the grill to a large serving platter. Let the chicken rest.

5. Meanwhile, make the sauce. In a medium bowl, stir together the **labneh**, the remaining **1 teaspoon harissa**, the juice of the remaining lemon half, and **¼ teaspoon salt**. Taste and add more harissa or lemon juice if you want.

6. Tear some **soft herbs** right over top for a pop of color and freshness. Throw everything on the table and let everyone serve themselves!

SMASHBURGER SAMMIES

½ small onion
1 pound 80/20 ground beef
Kosher salt and freshly ground
  black pepper
½ teaspoon garlic powder
6 tablespoons unsalted butter,
  at room temperature
Worcestershire sauce
8 slices rye (for patty melt
  vibes), white, or whole wheat
  bread
8 slices American cheese

LEARN
If your cheese doesn't melt, use this diner trick: Quickly add about 1 teaspoon of water to the skillet (away from the bread so it doesn't get soggy) and cover the pan. The steam will help the cheese melt.

BULK IT UP
This usually counts as a full meal for me (protein, carbs, vegetables!), but add some Obligatory Greens (see pages 248–249) if you must.

SERVES 4

These quick skillet burgers are somewhere between a smashburger, a patty melt, and grilled cheese. We went through a serious smashburger phase when I was pregnant with Calum, and the most eye-opening part of that experience was this: I like American cheese. My entire adult life, I'd thought myself too good for it, but no. It melts perfectly, it's creamy, and, IMO, it is a crucial element of a smashburger sammy.

1. Thinly slice the **onion**.

2. Divide the **ground beef** into 4 equal-size balls, then smoosh them into patties about 3 inches in diameter. Season all over with **salt**, **pepper**, and the **garlic powder**.

3. Melt **2 tablespoons of the butter** in a 12-inch cast-iron or stainless-steel skillet over medium-high heat. Add the patties to the skillet, then pile the onions on top of them. Tear off a small square of parchment paper and place it over one burger, then use a spatula to press the onions into the burger and flatten the patty as much as you can to get really thin, crispy edges. Remove the parchment and repeat with the remaining burgers. Season the onions with salt and pepper.

4. Cook until the bottom of each burger is dark brown and crispy, 2 to 3 minutes, then flip. If the onions didn't stick, try to scooch them under the meat as much as possible.

5. Shake a few dashes of **Worcestershire** onto each patty. Cook until the second side is golden brown, another 45 to 60 seconds, then transfer to a plate. Remove the skillet from the heat and wipe it out.

6. Spread a thin layer of butter onto one side of each slice of **bread**. Place 4 slices of bread buttered side down on a cutting board or plate and layer a slice of **American cheese** on top. Add a cooked patty, then another slice of cheese, then the second slice of bread, buttered side up.

7. Place the skillet over medium heat and cook the sandwiches until the bread is golden brown on the bottom, 1 to 2 minutes, then flip and cook until the cheese has melted and the bread is golden brown on the second side, 1 to 2 minutes more. Enjoy immediately.

PEANUTTY PORK & BRUSSELS

1 tablespoon untoasted sesame
 oil
1 pound ground pork
½ teaspoon kosher salt, plus
 more as needed
1 pound Brussels sprouts
4 garlic cloves
1 cup fresh cilantro leaves and
 tender stems
¼ cup low-sodium soy sauce
2 tablespoons rice vinegar
2 tablespoons creamy peanut
 butter
1 to 2 tablespoons sriracha
Toasted sesame seeds

LEARN
If your peanut butter is really thick, stir it together with the soy sauce before adding to the skillet.

SWAP
Any nut or seed butter will work in place of the peanut butter, and ground beef would be great in place of the pork. Shredded cabbage, green beans, red bell peppers, zucchini, or eggplant would all be excellent instead of the Brussels. Just cook the veg until tender—anything I just mentioned will take longer than sliced Brussels.

BULK IT UP
If you have leftover rice (or really, any grain) in the fridge, stir in a cup or so when you add the cilantro to bulk up this meal and feed more people—or make a fresh pot of rice and serve it under the pork.

SERVES 2 OR 3

Think of this one as more of a formula than a recipe. Ground meat + vegetables + a peanut sauce that comes together right in the skillet, no extra bowl required. That's why stir-fries are one of my favorite quick dishes to whip up with whatever's around. But this combination of fatty pork, shredded Brussels, and peanut sauce is on regular rotation at my house.

1. Warm the **sesame oil** in a large skillet over medium-high heat. When it shimmers, add the **ground pork** and **salt**. Cook, using a wooden spoon or spatula to break the pork up into tiny crumbles, until the pork is cooked through and no longer pink, 5 to 7 minutes.

2. Meanwhile, trim the **Brussels sprouts**, then halve them through their stems, place them flat side down, and slice them as thinly as you can—or throw them all in a food processor and pulse until they are shredded!

3. Add the sliced Brussels sprouts to the skillet and cook, stirring occasionally, until very tender, 3 to 4 minutes. Increase the heat as needed to get some nice brown color on the pork and Brussels. Use a Microplane to grate the **garlic** directly into the skillet and cook, stirring, until fragrant, about 30 seconds. Reduce the heat to medium. Finely chop the **cilantro**, stir it in, then scooch everything to one side of the skillet, leaving the other side empty.

4. Add the **soy sauce**, **vinegar**, **peanut butter**, and **1 tablespoon of the sriracha** to the empty side of the skillet and stir to dissolve the peanut butter (see Learn). Don't worry if bits of food get mixed in there. Once you've created a somewhat smooth sauce, stir it into the pork and Brussels to mix and coat evenly.

5. Taste and add more salt or sriracha as needed. Divide between plates, sprinkle with **sesame seeds**, and serve.

ROASTED SALMON & ASPARAGUS
with Dilly Sauce

5 dill sprigs
4 (6-ounce) salmon fillets
2 tablespoons extra-virgin
    olive oil
Kosher salt and freshly ground
    black pepper
2 lemons
2 bunches asparagus
½ cup mayonnaise
½ cup plain full-fat
    Greek yogurt
2 tablespoons Dijon mustard

TIP While it's not the environmentally conscious choice, I prefer the flavor and texture of farmed Atlantic salmon to wild salmon. It's fattier and thus less likely to dry out; plus, it's far less fishy-tasting.

LEARN Salmon is fine with the skin on or off, but buy the thickest fillets you can find and make sure they're all a comparable size for similar cooking times.

BULK IT UP Boil potatoes, eggs, and green beans and throw those on the platter, seasoned with salt and pepper, for a salmon Niçoise platter.

SERVES 4

My friend Lexie's entire family loves to cook, and they make an event out of every meal. Lunch is rarely a simple feat: The table is beautifully set, flowers are arranged, wine is poured. Randi, Lexie's mom, whipped up this lunch for us one afternoon at their home in Marin, California, arranged it on a big beautiful platter, and served it family style out on their patio. It looked like a spread straight out of *Sunset* magazine, but it didn't even take her 30 minutes. What makes it an especially fabulous meal is that it's just as delicious at room temperature as it is straight out of the oven.

1. Preheat the oven to 400°F.

2. Finely chop the **dill**. Arrange the **salmon** on a rimmed baking sheet. Drizzle **1 tablespoon of the olive oil** over the top, then season with a **big pinch each of salt** and **pepper**. Use a Microplane to zest half of **1 lemon** on top, then halve the lemon and squeeze over the juice from one half (reserve the other half for the asparagus). Sprinkle on 1 tablespoon of the dill and use your hands to rub it all over the salmon. Arrange the fillets on one side of the baking sheet, spacing them 1 inch apart.

3. Trim the **asparagus** and add it to the other side of the baking sheet. Drizzle with the remaining **1 tablespoon oil**, season with **½ teaspoon salt** and **¼ teaspoon pepper**, and toss to coat. They might be overlapping a bit—that's okay.

4. Roast the salmon and asparagus for 12 minutes, or until an instant-read thermometer registers 125°F for medium-rare (my preferred temp), 135°F for medium, or 140°F for medium-well. (Do not pass 140°F! This is where salmon gets dry and chalky.) Cook for a few minutes more if needed to reach your desired doneness.

5. In a small bowl, stir together the **mayonnaise**, **yogurt**, and **mustard**. Zest the whole second **lemon** directly into the bowl, then halve the lemon and squeeze in the juice. Season with **¼ teaspoon salt**, **¼ teaspoon pepper**, and the remaining dill.

6. Squeeze the juice from the reserved lemon half over the asparagus.

7. If you're serving immediately, divide the salmon and asparagus among four plates, drizzle with the sauce (or place it on the side), and dig in! If you're serving later, arrange everything on a pretty platter and refrigerate until mealtime. Pull it out of the fridge 30 minutes before eating to bring to room temperature.

SESAME CHILE FRIED EGG RICE BOWLS

1 cup sushi rice, rinsed
2 big handfuls of fresh spinach
2 tablespoons plus 1 teaspoon
   toasted sesame oil
Kosher salt
½ serrano chile
2 teaspoons sesame seeds
4 large eggs
2 teaspoons low-sodium soy
   sauce, plus more if needed

TIP This is a great meal to make when you have leftover rice: Just throw a scoop of rice into a skillet with a little sesame oil, spinach, and salt and sauté until the rice is warm and the spinach is wilted. Then proceed with the recipe from step 2.

SERVES 2

We aren't a huge "breakfast for dinner" family, but we are very into eggs for dinner. Yes, there's a difference! Eggs are an excellent protein that shouldn't be relegated to a.m. hours. Roasted veggies with a poached egg and pesto? Perfect dinner. Leftover pita with lots of crunchy veggies and a crispy fried egg? Bomb dinner! But my favorite nighttime egg special involves cooking up some sushi rice, slow frying eggs in sesame and soy sauce, and draping them over the soft sticky rice. The simplest, tastiest dinner of all.

1. Combine the **sushi rice** and **1½ cups water** in a small pot and bring it to a boil over high heat. Reduce the heat to low, cover, and cook until the liquid is completely absorbed and the rice is tender, 12 to 15 minutes. Add the **spinach** directly on top of the rice and drizzle it with **1 teaspoon of the sesame oil** and sprinkle with a **big pinch of salt**. Cover to steam until ready to eat.

2. Meanwhile, thinly slice the **serrano chile**. Remove the seeds if you're a spice wimp, then WASH YOUR HANDS to get those spicy oils off your fingers.

3. Heat the remaining **2 tablespoons sesame oil** in a large nonstick skillet over medium-low heat. Make 4 egg-size circles in the oil using ½ **teaspoon sesame seeds** and 4 slices of serrano each, then carefully and slowly crack the **eggs** directly over the tops—no worries if the seeds and serranos slide around a bit. Cover and cook for 3 minutes, then drizzle ½ **teaspoon soy sauce** over each egg, cover again, and cook until the whites are cooked through but the yolks are still runny, 1 to 2 minutes more.

4. Divide the spinach between two bowls and add a scoop of rice (you'll probably have leftover rice; see Tip). Top each with 2 fried eggs (they probably ran together and got stuck together—just use your spatula to separate them). Spoon any remaining chiles or sesame seeds from the skillet over the top.

5. When I eat this, I like to use a fork and knife to cut up the egg and mix everything together. Add more soy sauce if you like! Yum.

EVERYTHING-CRUSTED TUNA
with Snap Peas & Tahini-Jang Sauce

4 (4- to 6-ounce) tuna steaks
3 tablespoons low-sodium soy
  sauce
2 tablespoons sesame oil
  (toasted or not)
3 tablespoons everything bagel
  seasoning or sesame seeds,
  plus more as needed
1 tablespoon neutral oil
1 pound snap peas
2 garlic cloves
1 lime
3 tablespoons gochujang
2 tablespoons tahini (or any
  nut/seed butter)
1 tablespoon honey

LEARN
To get a smooth sauce, you might have to use a spoon to smoosh the tahini to help it incorporate. Add a tiny splash of water if needed to make it nice and drizzle-able.

Too spicy? Add a little more soy sauce and honey. Not thick enough? More tahini.

SWAP
Lots of swap possibilities for the snap peas! Snow peas or frozen peas will take less time, green beans will take a bit more time, and asparagus will take about the same amount of time as the snap peas.

SERVES 4

I always feel like an absolute mom beast when I whip up this meal on a random weeknight. It seems super bougie—like something you'd find on the menu at a white-tablecloth restaurant—but it's actually the fastest, simplest meal to prepare. A quick sear, a speedy sauté, and a really good sauce—done.

1. Rub the **tuna steaks** with **1 tablespoon of the soy sauce** and let them sit at room temperature while you heat your skillet, or for up to 30 minutes if you've got the time.

2. Heat a large skillet over medium-high heat. You want it really hot, which is why you're warming the pan while you prep the tuna.

3. Pat the marinated tuna steaks dry. Rub them all over with **1 tablespoon of the sesame oil** (or enough to lightly coat them). Pour the **everything bagel seasoning** onto a plate in an even layer, then press the tuna steaks into it until completely coated all over. You might need to add more seasoning to the plate as you work.

4. Add the **neutral oil** to the skillet, which should now be piping hot. Swirl the skillet to coat it with the oil, then add the tuna steaks. Cook until the seeds on the bottom are lightly golden, 1 to 2 minutes. Use tongs to flip the tuna and cook until the seeds on the second side are golden, 45 seconds to 1 minute more. Transfer the tuna to a cutting board to rest.

5. Meanwhile, return the skillet to medium heat (no need to wipe it out). Add the remaining **1 tablespoon sesame oil** to the skillet. When it shimmers, add the **snap peas**. Using a Microplane, grate in the **garlic** and the zest from half the **lime**; reserve the zested lime for the sauce. Cook, stirring occasionally, until the snap peas are crisp-tender, about 4 minutes. Stir in **1 tablespoon of the soy sauce** to coat. Remove the skillet from the heat.

6. In a jar, combine the **gochujang**, **tahini**, **honey**, and remaining **1 tablespoon soy sauce**. Halve the zested lime and squeeze in the juice. Cover with a lid and shake vigorously to combine.

7. Cut the tuna into ½-inch-thick slices and divide among four plates. Add the snap peas. Serve with the jar of tahini-jang sauce alongside for dipping and/or drizzling.

ANY FISH
with Saffron Cherry Tomatoes

1 large shallot
1 fennel bulb
4 garlic cloves
2 tablespoons unsalted butter
2 pints cherry tomatoes
Pinch of saffron (about
    20 threads)
Kosher salt and freshly ground
    black pepper
4 (6- to 8-ounce) fish fillets (I
    like cod or halibut)
4 pita breads

SWAP Feel free to swap in
any kind of tomato—just cut
them in half and squeeze out
their liquidy insides before
chopping into smaller pieces
to ensure you have a nice
thick tomato sauce.

Can't find saffron? Swap in
3/4 teaspoon ground turmeric.

LEARN Saffron and
tomatoes are wonderful
together. Try adding
a pinch of saffron to a
tomato pasta sauce, like
the tomato basil butter sauce
on page 233.

SERVES 4

Saffron is a spice most commonly used in Middle Eastern and Indian cuisine, and it is *special*, adding a subtle earthy sweetness to dishes. It is a pricy spice, but well worth it for the unique twist it adds anywhere you use it. Here, it brings sweet and acidic cherry tomatoes to life. The fish is poached right on top of the tomatoes, saving you an extra skillet to clean, and marrying all of those flavors. Serve this dish over rice, or simply with pita, like I do, for scooping up all of the saffron tomato goodness.

1. Thinly slice the **shallot** and the **fennel**. Mince the **garlic**.

2. Melt the **butter** in a 12-inch skillet over medium heat. Add the shallot, fennel, and garlic and cook, stirring often, until softened, about 4 minutes. Meanwhile, halve the **tomatoes**.

3. Add the tomatoes, **saffron, ¼ teaspoon salt**, and **¼ teaspoon pepper** to the skillet. Cook, stirring frequently, until the tomato juices begin to pool in the skillet, 3 to 4 minutes.

4. Add the **fish fillets**, nestling them into the tomatoes a bit. Season with a **big pinch each of salt** and **pepper**. Reduce the heat to medium-low, cover, and cook for 7 to 10 minutes, until the fish flakes easily with a fork.

5. Meanwhile, heat up the **pitas**. Throw them into a toaster oven or under the broiler in the oven for a few minutes. (You can brush them with some olive oil before warming, but I'm usually too lazy.)

6. Divide the fish and tomatoes among four plates and serve with the pitas alongside for scooping up the sauce.

THREE THINGS YOU CAN DO WITH RAMEN NOODLES

Ramen is the ultimate starting point for a 15-minute meal—the noodles cook in just a few minutes, they're cheap, and you can find them absolutely everywhere, from bougie specialty grocers to gas stations. Use good ol' Maruchan ramen or opt for a fancier ramen noodle if you please. Either way, you'll have a noodle shop–worthy bowl of saucy noods on your table in under 20 minutes.

VEGGIE PEANUT NOODS (PAGE 52)

SPICY RAMEN & SNAP PEA STIR-FRY (PAGE 51)

COCONUT CURRY
RAMEN & VEGGIE
NOODLE SOUP
(PAGE 50)

COCONUT CURRY RAMEN & VEGGIE NOODLE SOUP

2 red bell peppers

1 tablespoon neutral oil

8 ounces sliced mushrooms (any kind)

Kosher salt

2 to 4 tablespoons red curry paste

5 cups low-sodium vegetable stock

1 (13.5-ounce) can full-fat coconut milk

3 (3-ounce) packages instant Maruchan chicken or vegetable ramen noodles

1 (14- to 16-ounce) block extra-firm tofu

3 cups fresh spinach

1 lime

2 tablespoons fish sauce

1 tablespoon low-sodium soy sauce

TIP
I typically use tongs to serve the noodles and a ladle to serve the broth. Kind of annoying to use two utensils, but effective and efficient.

RIFF
For a chicken ramen noodle soup, cut a large boneless, skinless chicken breast into bite-size pieces and add it to the pot along with the peppers. Omit the tofu, or keep it for extra protein.

SERVES 4 TO 6

George and I have traveled around Thailand together twice: once when he was deployed to the Philippines during his time as a SEAL, and once when he did a business school internship in Bangkok. Both times, we visited Chiang Mai, a charming mountain town in the north, and both times we ate our weight in khao soi, a coconut curry noodle soup famous to the area that is spicy and pungent and creamy and a truly perfect bowl of food. Here's the version I make us when we're missing those misty, magical Thai mountains.

1. Thinly slice the **peppers**.

2. Warm the **oil** in a large pot over medium-high heat. When it shimmers, add the peppers, **mushrooms**, and ½ **teaspoon salt**. Cook, stirring occasionally (use tongs since you'll need them later), until the vegetables are slightly softened, 3 to 4 minutes. Stir in **2 tablespoons of the red curry paste** if you don't love spice, or up to 4 tablespoons if you can handle the heat. Cook, stirring frequently, until it darkens in color and starts to stick to the pot, another minute or two.

3. Stir in the **stock**, **coconut milk**, and **1 seasoning packet** from the ramen noodle packages (you can discard the others). Increase the heat to high and bring to a boil.

4. Meanwhile, drain the **tofu** and use your hands to squeeze the moisture out of it. If it breaks apart a bit, that's fine. When the soup is boiling, rip the tofu into bite-size pieces and add to the pot, along with the **ramen noodles** and **spinach**. Cook until the noodles are tender, smooshing everything down into the liquid, about 3 minutes. Cut the **lime** in half and squeeze in the juice. Stir in the **fish sauce** and **soy sauce**.

5. Divide among bowls and enjoy!

SPICY RAMEN & SNAP PEA STIR-FRY

12 ounces ramen noodles
5 ounces sugar snap peas
3 tablespoons unsalted
  butter
3 large eggs
3 tablespoons low-sodium
  soy sauce
1 tablespoon garlic powder
1 tablespoon sriracha
1 tablespoon brown sugar or
  honey
Finely chopped green
  things—scallions, fresh
  chives, or fresh cilantro,
  for serving

SWAP
This recipe is delicious with any skinny, long noodle. I especially love it with whole-wheat spaghetti, or with soba noodles to make it gluten-free. Or use 2 cups of cooked rice instead of noodles to make fried rice!

RIFF
Triple the snap peas and omit the noodles and eggs for a delightful veggie side dish.

SERVES 4 TO 6

My mom has an incredible green thumb and can make absolutely anything grow in her backyard in Winston-Salem, North Carolina. In the summertime, her garden beds are full of gigantic beanstalks overflowing with sugar snap peas that are so sweet, you can't help but eat them straight off the vine. We've had to come up with a lot of ways to cook all her sugar snaps over the years, and this noodle stir-fry is a family favorite—the sweet, snappy beans are the perfect contrast to the soft, chewy ramen.

1. Bring a large pot of water to a boil over high heat. Cook the **ramen noodles** according to the package instructions (discard the flavor packets if you're using instant ramen). Add the **snap peas** for the last 2 minutes of cooking. Drain in a colander.

2. Melt **1 tablespoon of the butter** in a large nonstick skillet over medium heat. Crack in the **eggs** and use a spatula to quickly stir to combine the whites and yolks. Cook, gently folding the eggs in onto themselves, until cooked through, 3 to 4 minutes.

3. Scooch the eggs to one side of the skillet and add the remaining **2 tablespoons butter** along with the **soy sauce**, **garlic powder**, **sriracha**, and **brown sugar** to the empty side of the skillet. Cook, stirring to combine the sauce and melt the sugar, about 2 minutes. Add the noodles and snap peas to the skillet and use tongs to toss them with the sauce and eggs, breaking the eggs up into small pieces and coating everything well.

4. Divide among bowls, garnish with **some green things**, and enjoy!

VEGGIE PEANUT NOODS

Kosher salt
10 ounces broccoli florets
   (3 to 4 cups)
9 ounces instant ramen
   noodles
1 cup frozen shelled
   edamame
½ cup creamy peanut butter
⅓ cup low-sodium soy sauce,
   plus more if needed
3 tablespoons rice vinegar,
   plus more if needed
1 tablespoon sriracha, plus
   1 to 2 tablespoons more if
   needed
1 tablespoon honey or sugar,
   plus more if needed
Toppings (optional): thinly
   sliced scallions, chopped
   cilantro, more sriracha,
   chopped toasted peanuts
   or almonds, sesame seeds,
   shredded carrots

TIP
Save any leftover sauce refrigerated in an airtight container up to 1 month. I love to steam frozen dumplings and broccoli at the same time, then serve with peanut sauce for dipping for a quickie meal.

LEARN
Here, you get to utilize one of my greatest time-saving cooking hacks by cooking the noodles and broccoli in the same pot: if a big pot of water is already boiling for pasta, use it to cook other things too! Steam veggies for tomorrow's lunch! Boil some eggs for the week!

SERVES 3 OR 4

These peanutty noodles were one of my family's hyperfixation meals during 2020's early lockdown days. We made them with all kinds of different noodles, nut butters, veggies, and meats. Now, any time I'm tasked with bringing a side dish to a dinner party or picnic, I bring these. Everyone is obsessed with them—not just us!

1. Bring a large pot of salted water to a boil over high heat.

2. Break the **broccoli florets** into 1-inch pieces. Add the broccoli, **ramen noodles**, and **edamame** to the boiling water and cook until the ramen is tender but maintains a nice chewy bite and the broccoli is tender, about 2 minutes. Drain in a colander, rinse with cold water, then shake to get excess water out.

3. Meanwhile, in a liquid measuring cup, whisk together the **peanut butter**, **soy sauce**, **vinegar**, **sriracha**, **honey**, and **1 tablespoon water**. It will seem very difficult to stir, but I promise it'll come together—just keep stirring! Add more water, 1 tablespoon at a time, as needed until you achieve a loose, drizzle-able consistency. Taste and add more soy sauce, vinegar, sriracha, and/or honey to your liking.

4. In a serving bowl, toss the noodles and vegetables with half of the peanut sauce until coated. If you like a super saucy dish, add more sauce. If the noods get too thick, add water, a tiny splash at a time, until the consistency is perfect. Divide among bowls and top with whatever you like and have handy.

PEANUT CHICKEN CHOP

2 tablespoons creamy peanut
  butter (I like Skippy)
2 tablespoons low-sodium soy
  sauce
1 tablespoon apple cider
  vinegar
1 tablespoon neutral oil
Sriracha
Honey
1 large romaine heart
1 cup shredded rotisserie
  chicken (or any cooked meat
  or tofu)
1 cup shredded carrots
½ cup shelled edamame

SERVES 1

When I'm in need of tons of protein, veggies, and greens but don't particularly *feel* like eating super healthy, I turn to this recipe format over and over again. The peanut dressing is salty-sweet and has a slight kick—it's positively addictive and will make you want to eat salad every day for the rest of your life. And let me tell you about the joy of popping store-bought shredded carrots into a salad. They add sweetness and crunch, and you don't have to do any work! They're always in my fridge.

1. In a large bowl, whisk together the **peanut butter**, **soy sauce**, **vinegar**, **oil**, and a squirt each of **sriracha** and **honey**.

2. Roughly chop the **romaine** (you should have about 3 cups) and add it to the bowl along with the **chicken**, **carrots**, and **edamame**. Toss well to coat. Enjoy!

TIP To make a big batch of this dressing (it'll keep in an airtight container in the refrigerator for up to 3 weeks), add 1 cup peanut butter, 1 cup soy sauce, 1/3 cup vinegar, 1/3 cup oil, 1 tablespoon sriracha, and 1 tablespoon honey to a jar. Shake to combine. If it's too thick, add a tiny splash of water and shake again.

RIFF Swap in leftover Crispy Miso Lime Tofu (page 60) for the chicken.

SWAP Cucumber, bell pepper, avocado, peanuts or cashews, and any other crisp, crunchy veg would be great thrown into this salad.

FOOLPROOF HERBY OMELET

5 large eggs
Handful of fresh soft herbs
(such as dill, basil, or
parsley), plus more for
serving
Kosher salt and freshly ground
black pepper
1 tablespoon unsalted butter
As much shredded cheese (any
type) as you want (I like 2 to
4 tablespoons)

LEARN
If you don't have a
lid that matches your pan, use
a baking sheet as a lid.

RIFF
Bagel sandwich:
2 teaspoons everything bagel
seasoning (instead of herbs) +
cheddar + ham

Caprese: fresh basil +
shredded mozzarella + sun-
dried tomatoes

Steak and eggs: fresh chives
+ 1/4 cup finely chopped
leftover steak + Parmesan

Easy cheesy: Skip the herbs
and fill the omelet with
Boursin cheese

BULK IT UP
Serve the
eggs with your choice of
Obligatory Greens (see pages
248-249)—I suggest the soft
greens.

SERVES 2

Omelets are both an art and a science—when young chefs are interviewing for positions in restaurants, they're often given a test of making a perfect omelet. But this recipe takes out all the guesswork. Just be sure your skillet is over medium-low heat, or even low heat if your stove tends to run hot—if the skillet is too hot, the eggs will get spongy instead of velvety and soft.

1. Warm a 10-inch nonstick skillet over medium-low heat. Seriously, start warming it now, before you do anything else.

2. Crack the **eggs** into a large bowl. Mince enough **herbs** to get 2 tablespoons and add them to the bowl along with ¼ **teaspoon salt** and a **big pinch of pepper**. Whisk until frothy and combined.

3. Melt the **butter** in the skillet, swirling the pan to coat the bottom. Pour the eggs into the skillet. Cover and cook until the eggs have ALMOST set, 3 to 6 minutes, rotating the skillet after 3 minutes.

4. Turn off the heat, then sprinkle the **cheese** over one half of the eggs. Fold the other side over the cheese. Cover and cook for 1 to 2 minutes more, until the cheese is melted.

5. Slide the omelet onto a plate and cut in half to share.

SAUCY EGGS
with Salty Olive Oil Bread

1 tablespoon extra-virgin olive
   oil, plus more as needed
5 ounces fresh spinach
Kosher salt and freshly ground
   black pepper
1 (28-ounce) jar marinara sauce
   or any pasta sauce
8 large eggs
4 ounces feta or goat cheese
4 large slices of good bread
Flaky sea salt
Parsley sprigs

LEARN
An extremely important tip for broiling: Turn the oven light on, sit down on your butt in front of the oven, and do not leave the oven's side! Bread goes from toasted to on fire very quickly. I know this is hard to do, but sitting still for a few minutes is easier than watching your beautiful loaf of bread come out of the oven as a lump of coal.

RIFF
Give your dish shakshuka vibes by stirring 1 1/2 teaspoons ground cumin, 1 teaspoon paprika, 1/2 teaspoon ground turmeric, and 1/4 teaspoon red pepper flakes into the sauce.

SWAP
Got salsa? Swap it in for the marinara to make Mexican-style saucy eggs!

SERVES 4 TO 6

I make saucy eggs for breakfast, lunch, or dinner at *least* once a week, using whatever sauce or tomato-based situation I have left over in the fridge. It's cozy while still being healthy, it's absurdly simple, and it's wildly satisfying. Whatever you do, don't skip the bread—scooping up perfect saucy, eggy, cheesy bites is essential.

1. Position a rack in the center of the oven and heat the broiler to high.

2. Warm the **olive oil** in a 12-inch skillet over medium heat. When it shimmers, add the **spinach** (in batches as needed to fit) and **a pinch each of salt** and **pepper**, and cook, stirring frequently, until it's wilted and all of the excess moisture has evaporated, 1 to 2 minutes. Add the **marinara sauce** and cook, stirring occasionally, until warmed through, about 4 minutes.

3. Use the back of a spoon to create 8 divots in the sauce, then crack **an egg** into each divot and sprinkle with **a pinch each of salt** and **pepper**. Crumble the **feta** over the top, avoiding the egg yolks as much as possible. Cover the pan and cook for 5 to 8 minutes, until the eggs have reached your desired doneness.

4. While the eggs steam, place the sliced **bread** on a rimmed baking sheet and coat with a decent layer of olive oil. Sprinkle with **flaky salt**. Broil for 1 to 2 minutes per side, until golden brown.

5. Use kitchen shears to snip some **parsley** over the saucy eggs. Serve in low bowls with the toasty bread alongside for dipping.

CRISPY MISO LIME TOFU

1 head butter lettuce
2 limes
2 tablespoons low-sodium soy
　　sauce
1 tablespoon white or yellow
　　miso
1 tablespoon rice vinegar
2 tablespoons honey
½ teaspoon ground ginger
½ teaspoon garlic powder
¼ teaspoon red pepper flakes
1 (14- to 16-ounce) block extra-
　　firm tofu
3 tablespoons neutral oil, plus
　　more as needed
Toppings (optional): sesame
　　seeds, sriracha, fresh herbs,
　　chopped peanuts

SERVES 2

Sometimes greatness is born out of necessity, which is how this recipe
came to be. George and I were hosting friends for dinner, serving Bo Ssam
(page 238). Just before we brought the food out, I remembered one of our
guests was a vegetarian. I happened to have a block of tofu in the fridge,
but with no time to press it, I just started squeezing the moisture out of it
with my hands over the sink. I then cooked it over super high heat to get it
crispy, stirred in a simple pantry sauce, and the rest is history. We were all
obsessed—all of the pork lovers at the table kept stealing the tofu!

1. Pull the leaves off the head of **butter lettuce**, then wash and dry them.
   Cut the **limes** in half.

2. In a medium bowl or liquid measuring cup, stir together the juice of 1 lime,
   the **soy sauce**, **2 tablespoons water**, the **miso**, **vinegar**, **honey**, **ginger**,
   garlic powder, and **red pepper flakes**. Smash the miso against the side of
   the cup to be sure it incorporates to make a smooth sauce.

3. Warm your largest skillet over medium-high heat. Working over the sink,
   remove the **tofu** from the container, pour out any liquid, and reserve the
   container. Use your hands to break the tofu into a few pieces and squeeze
   out as much liquid as you possibly can. This won't be pretty! It'll break
   apart into little bits. That's perfect, you're doing it right. When you feel
   like you've squeezed all the liquid you can out of the tofu, place it back in
   the container it came in.

4. Add the **oil** to the super hot skillet. When it shimmers, add the squeezed,
   crumbled tofu in an even layer and let it sit, undisturbed, for 3 minutes.
   Give it a stir, then let it sit for 3 minutes more. It should start to look
   crispy and golden brown at this point. Keep going with this stir-and-
   sit pattern once or twice more, adding more oil to the pan as needed,
   until the tofu is crispy all over. Add the sauce and stir rapidly until it's all
   absorbed into the tofu, not even a minute. Turn off the heat.

5. To serve, fill the lettuce leaves with crispy tofu and any toppings you like,
   including sesame seeds, sriracha, chopped fresh herbs, chopped peanuts,
   or any combination thereof. Squeeze the juice from the remaining lime
   over top just before eating.

CANNELLINI CAPRESE WITH BURRATA

¼ cup extra-virgin olive oil
3 tablespoons red wine vinegar
2 teaspoons honey
Kosher salt and freshly ground
   black pepper
2 garlic cloves
1 (15-ounce) can white beans,
   such as cannellini or navy,
   drained and rinsed
2 pints cherry tomatoes
¼ small red onion
¾ cup fresh basil leaves
1 large avocado
2 (4-ounce) burrata balls,
   drained and at room
   temperature
Bread (any type!), for serving

TIP
The tomatoes will give off a lot of liquid, so if you have leftovers, pour that off before enjoying a second time so the salad doesn't get soggy.

LEARN
A rule to live by: If your bread is really good, you probably don't need to toast it. But if it's grocery store bread, a drizzle of olive oil and a blast under the broiler will bring it to life.

BULK IT UP
Add a big handful of mixed greens or arugula to make it a leafy green salad.

RIFF
Make it a handheld appetizer situation by making crostini! Toast a bunch of baguette slices, smear them with good ricotta, then pile a spoonful of the caprese salad on top.

SERVES 4 AS A MAIN OR 6 AS AN APPETIZER

Summer of 2020 saw George's debut as an amateur tomato farmer. We had just moved into our home in Carmel Valley, California, and while my version of nesting was hanging window treatments and art, his was filling up every square inch of usable soil with tomato plants. We have countless photos of our son Mattis, then eighteen months old, sitting in the yard eating tomatoes like they were apples, warm tomato juice dribbling down his pudgy body and pooling into every roll. We must have eaten five hundred caprese salads, to which I finally started adding white beans to make it a complete meal. This is that perfect bite of summer.

1. In a large bowl, whisk together the **olive oil**, **vinegar**, **honey**, **2 teaspoons salt**, and ½ **teaspoon pepper**. Use a Microplane to grate in the **garlic**. Add the **beans** and use a fork to lightly smash them; they should still hold their shape.

2. Halve or quarter the **tomatoes** and place them in a colander. Sprinkle with a **big pinch of salt** and toss, then leave them in the sink to drain for a bit.

3. Meanwhile, thinly slice the **onion** and gently tear the **basil leaves**. Add both to the dressing. Dice the **avocado** and add it to the bowl as well. Add the drained tomatoes to the salad and gently toss to combine. Taste and season with more salt and pepper if needed. Divide the salad among four bowls. Tear the **burrata balls** in half, placing a half on top of each salad.

4. Slice the **bread** and serve alongside. (I like to spoon a little burrata and salad over a baguette slice and eat it like bruschetta!)

30 MINUTES

EASY & ELEGANT STEAK SALAD

1 (8-ounce) sirloin steak (or 2 steaks if you're big meat eaters!)

Kosher salt and freshly ground black pepper

4 ounces diced pancetta

2 tablespoons pine nuts

4 dates

4 cups arugula, frisée, radicchio (torn), or a combination

Juice of ½ lemon, plus more as needed

Extra-virgin olive oil

½ ounce Parmesan cheese (or blue cheese if you dig it)

RIFF
Easy & Elegant Chicken Salad: Use bacon instead of pancetta, walnuts instead of pine nuts, chicken breast instead of steak, balsamic instead of lemon juice, yellow raisins instead of dates, and avocado instead of Parm. Same concept, totally different salad. Still hits.

SERVES 2

When my grandfather really loved a meal that my grandmother cooked, he used to exclaim, "Do you know how much we would have paid for this at a restaurant?!" It's still one of the highest culinary compliments in my family, and we all get a real kick out of it any time someone says it. This is a meal worthy of the acclaim. Crisp pancetta, toasty pine nuts, perfectly cooked steak, sweet and chewy dates, and a touch of salty Parm. It hits every note, and it sure would be expensive at a restaurant.

1. Pat the **steak** dry, then season generously with **salt** and **pepper**.

2. Place the **pancetta** in a 12-inch cast-iron or stainless-steel skillet and cook over medium-high heat, stirring occasionally, until the pancetta is crispy, about 5 minutes. When it's almost ready (around minute 3 or 4), add the **pine nuts** to the skillet to toast in the rendered pancetta fat. When the pancetta is crisp and the nuts are golden brown, turn off the heat and use a slotted spoon to transfer them to a paper towel–lined plate to drain.

3. Return the skillet to medium-high heat (no need to wipe it out). Add the steak and cook until golden and an instant-read thermometer registers 130°F (for medium-rare), 3 to 4 minutes per side. Transfer the steak to a cutting board to rest.

4. Meanwhile, pit and chop the **dates**.

5. In a large bowl, toss the **arugula** with the **lemon juice, 1½ tablespoons extra-virgin olive oil, ¼ teaspoon salt**, and a **little bit of pepper**. Taste and add more of whichever of these it needs for the greens to taste delicious to you.

6. You could just throw everything else into the bowl here, but this meal deserves your two extra minutes for presentation (and we deserve nice things!). Thinly slice the steak. Divide the dressed arugula between two plates along with the pancetta, pine nuts, and dates. Use a vegetable peeler to shave the **Parm** into big ribbons on top of each plate. Add the steak on top. Serve, and receive compliments.

CREAMY DIJON PORK TENDERLOIN & MUSHROOMS

4 tablespoons extra-virgin
   olive oil, plus more as needed
1½ pounds thinly sliced
   mushrooms
Kosher salt and freshly ground
   black pepper
1 medium red or yellow onion
1 (1- to 1½-pound) pork
   tenderloin
½ teaspoon garlic powder, or 2
   garlic cloves, minced
¾ cup half-and-half
1 heaping tablespoon Dijon
   mustard
1 cup fresh parsley leaves and
   tender stems
2 teaspoons apple cider
   vinegar or red wine vinegar

LEARN
Silver skin is
connective tissue that will
make your tenderloin chewy and
tough instead of tender. To
remove it, press the tip of a
sharp knife under the shiny,
silver skin at one end of
the tenderloin. Slowly guide
the knife from one end of
the tenderloin to the other,
pulling away the silver skin
with the other hand as you
move.

BULK IT UP
Serve this
one over herby couscous (see
page 203) or over egg noodles
to lean into the stroganoff-
ness. Yum.

SERVES 4

I love a big bright bowl full of beautiful produce just as much as the next gal, but ya know what? Sometimes beige food is the best food. This one-skillet meal is packed with lean protein and veggies, while also bringing cozy, creamy decadence. It has stroganoff vibes, with a plucky sauce and lots and lots of mushrooms to go around.

1. Warm **2 tablespoons of the olive oil** in your largest nonstick skillet over medium-high heat. When it shimmers, add the **mushrooms** and stir to coat in oil. Spread them into an even layer and cook, undisturbed, for 3 minutes, then stir, spread evenly again, and cook, undisturbed, for 3 minutes more. Add more oil if the skillet gets too dry. Repeat until the mushrooms are browned, 6 to 9 minutes total, then season with **¼ teaspoon salt** and **a few grinds of pepper**. Transfer the mushrooms to a bowl.

2. While the mushrooms cook, thinly slice the **onion**. Remove the silver skin (see Learn) from the **pork tenderloin**, cut the meat crosswise into ½-inch-thick rounds, then cut each round piece into a half-moon.

3. Return the empty mushroom skillet to medium-high heat (no need to wipe it out). Add the remaining **2 tablespoons olive oil**. When it shimmers, add the onion and pork. Season with **1½ teaspoons salt**, **a few grinds of pepper**, and the **garlic powder**. Cook, stirring occasionally, until the pork is almost cooked through, about 4 minutes. Add the mushrooms and any juices that have collected, the **half-and-half**, and the **mustard**. Cook, stirring, until the sauce thickens and wraps itself around the pork and mushrooms, 2 to 3 minutes.

4. While the pork cooks, finely chop the **parsley**.

5. Stir in the chopped parsley and the **vinegar**. Divide among four bowls and enjoy.

ONE-SKILLET BALSAMIC MUSHROOM BRACED CHICKEN

1½ to 2 pounds boneless, skinless chicken breast tenders
Kosher salt and freshly ground black pepper
1 large shallot
8 parsley sprigs
5 tablespoons extra-virgin olive oil, plus more for drizzling
1 pound sliced mushrooms
1 loaf crusty bread
3 tablespoons all-purpose flour
1½ cups low-sodium chicken stock
½ cup dry white wine (I like sauvignon blanc)
2 tablespoons balsamic vinegar
2 teaspoons brown sugar
8 thyme sprigs
2 tablespoons unsalted butter

LEARN
Chicken tenders have a tough ligament that runs through them vertically. To remove it, grab the end (it looks like a white string) with a clean towel, then put the tines of a fork on either side of it and pull the ligament through the tines. It might rip the chicken a bit, but no big deal. Also, no big deal if you don't feel like doing this; I often skip this step.

BULK IT UP
This chicken would also be delicious over cauliflower mash (see page 78), Plain Jane couscous (see page 203), or rice.

SERVES 4

Announcement: Chicken breast tenders are really freaking underrated. They're a cheap cut of meat that doesn't get nearly enough love. If you can't find them, just cut chicken breasts into 1-inch-thick strips. In this dish, the meat becomes tender and juicy with so very little effort. The sauce they're plunked in is decadent and tangy, and you absolutely have to scoop it all up with lots of really good bread.

1. Preheat the oven to 400°F.

2. Season the **chicken tenders** generously with **salt** and **pepper** (see Learn). Mince the **shallot**. Finely chop the **parsley**.

3. Warm **2 tablespoons of the olive oil** in a 12-inch skillet over medium-high heat. Pat the chicken very dry. When the oil shimmers, add the chicken and cook until a nice golden brown crust appears, 2 to 3 minutes per side (it won't be totally cooked through yet). Transfer to a plate.

4. Return the skillet to medium-high heat (no need to wipe it out) and add the remaining **3 tablespoons olive oil**.

5. When it shimmers, add the **mushrooms** and stir to coat in oil. Spread them into an even layer and cook, undisturbed, for 3 minutes, then stir, spread evenly again, and cook, undisturbed, for 3 minutes more. Stir in the minced shallots. Add more oil if the skillet gets too dry. Repeat until the mushrooms are browned, 6 to 9 minutes total, then season with **¼ teaspoon salt** and **a few grinds of pepper**.

6. While the mushrooms cook, cut eight 1-inch-thick slices of **bread** and place them on a baking sheet. Drizzle generously with **olive oil** and sprinkle with **salt**. Bake for 10 to 12 minutes, until golden brown on the outside but still very tender and chewy.

7. Back to the skillet: Add the **flour** and cook, stirring, until everything looks pasty and no white specks remain, about 30 seconds. Stir in the **stock**, **wine**, **vinegar**, **brown sugar**, **½ teaspoon salt**, and the **thyme**. Cook until the sauce has thickened, 4 to 6 minutes. Reduce the heat to medium-low and pluck out and discard the thyme sprigs. Stir in the **butter** to melt. Nestle the chicken and any collected juices into the sauce. Simmer until the chicken is cooked through, 3 to 4 minutes.

8. Serve the chicken and mushrooms in low bowls with the toasted bread alongside for sopping up that delicious sauce.

SAUCY SESAME BEEF NOODLES

Kosher salt
1 pound spaghetti (or any long
 noodle)
1 medium yellow onion
1 (2-inch) piece fresh ginger
4 garlic cloves
4 tablespoons sesame oil
1 pound shaved beef (or
 1 pound sirloin or rib eye
 steak, sliced as thinly as
 possible)
1 (10-ounce) bag shredded
 carrots
⅓ cup low-sodium soy sauce
¼ cup rice vinegar
2 tablespoons tahini
2 tablespoons sriracha, sambal
 oelek, or gochujang
1½ tablespoons honey
1 tablespoon fish sauce
Toppings (optional): chopped
 fresh cilantro and/or basil,
 sesame seeds, chopped
 peanuts, more sriracha

LEARN
You don't always
have to dirty up a separate
bowl to make your sauce.
Just dump all of the sauce
ingredients straight into the
center of the skillet and stir
together as best you can. No
worries if it's not totally
homogeneous; it'll all come
together in the end.

SERVES 4 TO 6

Saucy noods are reliably a balm to my soul at the end of a long, crappy day. I keep an absurd number of different kinds of noodles on hand at all times, and I especially love spaghetti for its ability to swing into a dish with Italian or Asian flavors. You don't typically think of pasta as a great meal-prep option, but this dish truly gets better and better as it sits in the fridge for a day or two absorbing the sauce, so don't be afraid to make it if you're only cooking for one or two people.

1. Bring a large pot of salted water to a boil. Add the **spaghetti** and cook according to the package instructions. Scoop out **1 cup of the pasta cooking water**, then drain the pasta and return it to the pot.

2. Meanwhile, thinly slice the **onion**. Grate the **ginger** (no need to peel it first) and **garlic**.

3. Warm **2 tablespoons of the sesame oil** in a large skillet over medium-high heat. When it shimmers, add the sliced onion and cook, stirring often, until softened, about 4 minutes. Add the remaining **2 tablespoons sesame oil**, then when it shimmers, add the **beef**, peeling apart the pieces, the **carrots**, and the ginger and garlic, and cook, stirring often, until the steak is almost cooked through but still slightly pink in the center, 3 to 4 minutes. Scooch everything over to one side of the skillet.

4. To the empty side of the skillet, add ½ cup of the cooking water, the **soy sauce**, **vinegar**, **tahini**, **sriracha**, **honey**, and **fish sauce**. Stir it all together until combined, then stir it together with the beef and carrots. Cook until the sauce thickens a bit, another minute.

5. Transfer everything from the skillet into the pot with the pasta and stir to coat. Add more splashes of cooking water as needed—the sauce should be glossy and stick to the noodles. Taste and add salt if needed.

6. Divide among bowls and serve with any **toppings** that make you happy.

BLACKENED SALMON & CABBAGE

Extra-virgin olive oil
2 tablespoons jerk or Cajun
    seasoning
Kosher salt
1 lime
4 (6-ounce) skin-on salmon
    fillets
1 small head napa cabbage
¾ teaspoon garlic powder
2 tablespoons apple cider
    vinegar
1 tablespoon unsalted butter

RIFF
So many flavor
combinations will be delicious
here. Try rubbing the salmon
with curry powder and cumin,
then adding extra curry
powder, soy sauce, fish sauce,
and lime juice to the cabbage
while cooking it for a curried
salmon and cabbage spin.

BULK IT UP
Add a
side of coconut rice (see
page 188).

SERVES 4

George and I are co-presidents of the Cabbage Appreciation Club—there's always a head of cabbage in our refrigerator waiting to be turned into a cold crunchy salad, or else cooked into caramelized, tender submission. I especially love cooking it when I have people over for dinner because they absolutely lose their marbles: "This is CABBAGE?!" This is one of our very favorite weeknight meals for when we are trying to eat healthily but still want something truly delicious.

1. In a large bowl or zip-top bag, combine **2 tablespoons olive oil**, the **jerk seasoning**, and **¼ teaspoon salt**. Cut the **lime** in half and squeeze in the juice. Add the **salmon** and turn to coat. If you have the time, let marinate in the refrigerator for up to 24 hours, but it'll still be great if you don't.

2. Warm your largest skillet over medium-high heat for 4 minutes. Remove the salmon from the marinade, reserving the marinade, and place the salmon skin side down in the pan. Cook until a blackened crust forms on the bottom of the fish, 5 to 8 minutes. Using a thin spatula, flip the salmon, reduce the heat to low, and cook until an instant-read thermometer registers 130°F for medium-rare or 145°F for well-done, 2 to 4 minutes more. Transfer the salmon to a plate and cover with foil.

3. While the salmon cooks, thinly slice the **cabbage** into ¼-inch-thick ribbons (you'll have about 10 cups).

4. Place the skillet from the salmon (no need to wipe it out) over high heat. Add the cabbage (it'll seem like way too much, but it'll cook down!), the reserved marinade, **garlic powder**, and **¼ teaspoon salt** and cook, stirring occasionally, until tender and browned, 6 to 8 minutes. Stir in the **vinegar** and **butter** to melt. Taste and add more salt as desired.

5. Divide the salmon fillets and cabbage among plates and serve.

DILLY CHOP
with Salt & Vinegar Chippies

⅔ cup extra-virgin olive oil
¼ cup apple cider vinegar
2 tablespoons mayonnaise
1 tablespoon honey
1 tablespoon Dijon mustard
Kosher salt and freshly ground
 black pepper
2 romaine hearts
1 cup pitted Castelvetrano
 olives
6 ounces Manchego cheese
4 ounces salami
½ cup roasted, salted pistachios
1 bunch dill
A few handfuls of salt and
 vinegar chips

LEARN
This recipe will teach you how to make my all-time fave vinaigrette. Start with my recipe, then adjust it to your liking (more vinegar? more honey?) and jot down your alterations in the margins of this page. Bam: You just invented your "house vinaigrette." Keep it in a big jar in the fridge at all times for easy salad-ing.

SWAP
Make like Stationæry and swap in seasonal greens and veggies. I went in one July and there were thinly sliced raw green beans in the salad. One winter they threw really thinly slivered raw beets in there. Fennel would be excellent. Anything crisp and crunchy will do well here.

SERVES 4

Our friends Anthony and Alissa Carnazzo own and operate Stationæry, the most charming neighborhood restaurant in downtown Carmel-by-the-Sea. Their menu changes with the seasons, but one thing that never leaves it is the Farmer's Salad with seasonal greens and veggies, dill, sheep's milk cheese, pistachios, and cider vinaigrette. Even with a menu full of so many beautiful options, I can't resist getting this salad almost every time I go in—it's completely addicting. I've added something I know they'll approve of because they love mixing "slutty" (as Anthony would say) ingredients into their high-brow menu: salt and vinegar chips as croutons.

1. In a jar with a lid, combine the **olive oil**, **vinegar**, **mayonnaise**, **honey**, **mustard**, **1 teaspoon salt**, and **several grinds of pepper**. Twist closed and shake vigorously until combined, about 30 seconds. Taste and adjust the seasonings as desired.

2. Thinly slice the **romaine** (you should have about 6 cups) and combine it in a large bowl with a **big pinch each of salt** and **pepper**.

3. Chop the **olives**, shred the **Manchego**, and thinly slice the **salami** and add them to the bowl, along with the **pistachios**. Chop the **dill** and add it to the bowl along with your desired amount of dressing—I recommend starting with ⅓ cup—and use tongs to toss and coat.

4. Crumble the **salt and vinegar chips** over top of the entire salad, like a blanket of chippy snow. Serve immediately.

LEMONY HERBY TURKEY PATTIES
with Cauliflower Mash & Sautéed Spinach

FOR THE CAULIFLOWER MASH
1 (12-ounce) bag cauliflower rice
2 garlic cloves
2 tablespoons sour cream
½ cup freshly grated Parmesan cheese
Kosher salt and freshly ground black pepper

FOR THE TURKEY PATTIES
½ cup fresh parsley leaves and tender stems
1 pound ground turkey
⅓ cup panko breadcrumbs
¼ cup freshly grated Parmesan cheese, plus more for serving
1 large egg
2 tablespoons sour cream
1 teaspoon kosher salt
Freshly ground black pepper
2 garlic cloves
1 lemon
2 tablespoons extra-virgin olive oil

FOR THE SPINACH
1 pound mature fresh spinach
1 tablespoon extra-virgin olive oil
½ teaspoon kosher salt

RIFF Roll the turkey into balls instead of flattening into patties and you've got meatballs! Bake at 425°F for 15 minutes.

SHORTCUT Grab frozen Italian meatballs and serve them with the cauliflower mash and sautéed spinach for a quickie protein- and veggie-packed meal.

SERVES 4

These flavorful patties are a great alternative to plain ol' chicken breasts for an easy weeknight protein. They're full of bright, herby flavor, and they're simple to throw together. This cauliflower mash is a favorite healthy-ish side dish that serves as part sauce, part side—I like to swoop up a little bit of the mash onto each bite.

1. **Start the cauliflower mash:** In a large microwave-safe bowl, combine the **cauliflower rice**, **garlic cloves**, and **¼ cup water**. Cover with a plate and microwave on high for 12 minutes. Carefully remove the plate (it's gonna be HOT!), pour off any liquid in the bowl, and squish the cauliflower with a fork. If it's not easy to mash, keep cooking in 1-minute intervals until it is.

2. **Make the turkey patties:** Finely chop the **parsley** and place most of it in a large bowl (reserve the rest for serving). Add the **ground turkey, panko, Parm, egg, sour cream, salt,** and **a few grinds of pepper**. Grate in the **garlic** and the zest of the **lemon** (reserve the zested lemon for the spinach). Use your hands to mix well but gently, then create four (½-inch-thick) patties. Gently form your patties to ensure they will be super tender and juicy.

3. Warm the **olive oil** in a 12-inch nonstick skillet over medium-high heat. When it shimmers, add the patties and cook until golden brown all over, 4 to 5 minutes per side. Transfer to a plate and tent with foil to keep warm.

4. **Make the spinach:** Halve the zested lemon. In the hot skillet (no need to clean it first), off the heat, combine the **spinach, olive oil,** and **salt** and squeeze in the juice from one lemon half. Give it a big stir and cover while you finish cooking the rest of the meal.

5. Turn your attention back to the cauliflower: You can either make a rough mash by just mashing everything right in the bowl, or you can transfer everything to a blender and blend for about 30 seconds to create a smooth puree. Whichever adventure you choose, add the **sour cream, Parm,** a tiny squeeze of lemon juice (about 2 teaspoons/one-quarter of the lemon remaining from the spinach), **¼ teaspoon salt,** and **a few grinds of pepper**. Add a splash of **water** (or stock, if you have some on hand) if needed to loosen it up as you mash or blend. Taste and adjust the seasonings as needed.

6. Divide the cauliflower mash among four plates. Uncover the steamed spinach and give it a big stir, then divide it among the plates, too. Add a patty to each. Garnish the whole plate with a nice sprinkle of parsley and more Parm.

PARM-CRUSTED TUNA MELTS

3 (5-ounce) cans water-packed tuna, drained well
¾ cup bread-and-butter pickles, plus 3 tablespoons brine
⅓ cup mayonnaise, plus more for spreading
½ teaspoon kosher salt
Freshly ground black pepper
8 slices sourdough bread
8 deli slices sharp cheddar cheese
¼ cup freshly grated Parmesan cheese

TIP
I always make my tuna salad directly in a storage container because I count on having leftovers. If you, like me, don't use all of the tuna salad at once, you might find you need to add more mayo and/or pickle brine to the leftovers the next day—the tuna can get a bit dry as it sits.

SWAP
You can swap butter for mayo on the outside of the bread (butter is more flavorful, but I love how beautifully a smear of mayo toasts on bread), use canned or finely chopped cooked chicken if you don't love tuna, and dill pickles if you don't love B&Bs.

SERVES 4

This tuna salad is quick and dirty: no fuss, all glory. If you want, add some Dijon, maybe some minced shallot, even some celery (if you must). But you don't need any of that for it to be a total dinnertime win. Slap it onto some high-quality sourdough smooshed between cheddar cheese slices, and *whoa*.

1. In a large bowl, use a fork to mash up the **tuna** completely—no big chunks should remain. Dice the **pickles** and add them to the bowl, along with the **brine**, **mayonnaise**, **salt**, and **a few grinds of pepper**.

2. Lay out **4 slices of the bread** on your countertop and place a slice of **cheddar** on each. Spoon your desired amount of tuna salad onto each, then top with a second slice of **cheddar**.

3. Warm your largest skillet (or griddle if you have one!) over medium heat for 3 to 4 minutes. Top the sandwiches with the remaining **4 slices of bread**. Spread a thin layer of **mayo** over the tops of the sandwiches, then sprinkle with half the **Parmesan**, pressing to adhere. Working in batches as needed, gently place the sandwiches, Parm side down, into the skillet. While they're in there, spread mayo over the slices of bread that are now on top, then add the remaining Parm.

4. Cook the sandwiches, pressing down gently every once in a while with a spatula, until the bottoms are toasty and crispy and the bottom slice of cheddar has melted, 3 to 5 minutes.

5. Carefully flip the sandwiches and cook until toasty and crispy and melty on the second side, 2 minutes or so more.

6. Transfer the sandwiches to a cutting board and let them rest for a few minutes; if you cut right in, everything will just ooze out. When it's time, slice your melts in half and enjoy.

more
MELTY
SANDWICHES
that totally count as dinner

COOK THESE IN A SKILLET OVER MEDIUM HEAT FOR A FEW MINUTES PER SIDE. ALL THESE COMBOS WOULD ALSO MAKE EXCELLENT KING'S HAWAIIAN SLIDERS (SEE PAGE 136). FEEL FREE TO GIVE ANY OF THESE THE CRISPY-PARM TREATMENT (SEE PAGE 81); IT'S NEVER A BAD IDEA.

ITALIAN STALLION
Sourdough + pesto + mayo + salami + pepperoni + mortadella + banana peppers + provolone

HAM & JAM
Whole wheat + mayo + raspberry (or any berry) jam + ham + white cheddar

TURKEY PESTO
White bread + mayo + pesto + turkey + Swiss + pesto on the outside of the bread too (it crisps up and is so delicious)

HAM & PICKLES
Whole wheat + Dijon mustard + mayo + ham + bread-and-butter pickles + cheddar or American cheese

CHICKEN APPLE BRIE
Sourdough + honey mustard + shredded chicken + thinly sliced green apple + Brie + arugula + butter on the outside of the bread

TOASTY ROASTY
Some sort of seedy-wheaty bread + mayo + a little horseradish smeared into the mayo + mozzarella + roast beef + peperoncini

PROSCIUTTO PESTO CAPRESE
Sourdough + pesto + mozzarella + fresh tomatoes + sun-dried tomatoes + arugula + prosciutto

SAUSAGE & KALE PASTA

Kosher salt
1 pound rotini or fusilli pasta
1 pound mild or hot Italian
sausage, casings removed
1 bunch curly kale
½ cup sun-dried tomatoes
4 garlic cloves
1 tablespoon tomato paste
1 cup heavy cream
1 cup low-sodium chicken stock
½ cup freshly grated Parmesan
cheese, plus more for
serving

TIP
Get a head start by making the creamy sausage and kale sauce entirely ahead of time. Let it cool, then throw it in the refrigerator right in the pot. Warm it up over medium heat and add the pasta when it's time to eat.

LEARN
The most efficient way to stem kale leaves is this: Grab the stem by the bottom, peel the leaves up and away from the bottom just a bit, then pull the leaf by its stem through your fingers to strip the leaf from the stem.

SERVES 4 TO 6

We renovated our Carmel Valley home in 2023 and rented a house next door to our good friends the Harringtons for several months while we had to be out of ours. They have three kids, and we have three kids, so it was a summer of nonstop Nerf gun wars, scooter rides to the beach, trampoline games, and "compound dinners." Pleasing six kids and four adults with one meal is no easy feat, but once I discovered how much the compound loved this pasta, I stuck with it. It's creamy, super flavorful with little effort, and a universal crowd-pleaser (yes, even with the kale!).

1. Bring a large pot of salted water to a boil. Cook the pasta to al dente according to the package instructions. Scoop out **1 cup of the pasta cooking water**, then drain the pasta and set aside.

2. Warm a large Dutch oven over medium-high heat. Add the **sausage** and cook, breaking it up with a wooden spoon, until browned, about 8 minutes. Drain off all but a spoonful of grease.

3. Meanwhile, stem the **kale**. Chop the leaves into small (2-ish-inch) pieces. Thinly slice the **sun-dried tomatoes** and **garlic**.

4. Reduce the heat to medium and add the sun-dried tomatoes, garlic, and **tomato paste**. Cook, stirring frequently, until the tomato paste darkens in color and begins sticking to the pot, about 1 minute. Add the kale and a splash of the reserved pasta cooking water and cook, stirring often, until the kale is tender, 2 to 3 minutes.

5. Stir in the **cream**, **stock**, **Parm**, and **½ teaspoon salt**. Cook for 3 minutes to allow the sauce to thicken. Add the cooked pasta to the pot with the sauce and cook, stirring, for 2 to 3 minutes, until the sauce is clinging to the pasta and everything is thick and creamy. If it gets too thick, stir in a splash of the reserved pasta cooking water.

6. Serve the pasta in low bowls with more grated Parm over the top.

SHEET PAN PESTO HALIBUT & GREEN BEANS

1 lemon
1 pound green beans
Extra-virgin olive oil
Kosher salt and freshly ground
    black pepper
4 (6-ounce) halibut fillets
4 tablespoons pesto

RIFF
Green beans almondine:
Melt 2 tablespoons butter in a
skillet, add a minced shallot,
a minced garlic clove, and 1/4
cup slivered almonds. Stir
until the almonds are toasted.
Toss this mixture into the
cooked green beans after they
roast.

Crunchy pesto halibut: Melt
3 tablespoons butter in a
microwave-safe bowl and stir
in 1/2 cup panko breadcrumbs
and a pinch of salt. Press the
breadcrumbs into the pesto
when it's on top of the fish
and continue the recipe as
written.

Caesar roasted halibut:
Marinate the halibut overnight
in 1 cup of Caesar dressing
(I like Ken's Steakhouse,
honestly). Roast as written,
then serve the fish and green
beans with the remaining
dressing.

SERVES 4

One summer, George went on an epic weeklong fishing trip to Alaska with some old SEAL friends and came home with enough halibut to last us a lifetime. We've Bubba Gumped the heck out of halibut, cooking it every imaginable way (you can barbecue it, boil it, broil it, bake it, sauté it . . .). This simple sheet pan meal is the one we come back to over and over—it's impressive with very little effort.

1. Preheat the oven 400°F. Line a rimmed baking sheet with parchment paper.

2. Zest the **lemon**; set the zested lemon aside for serving. On the prepared baking sheet, toss the **green beans** (trim them first, if you must—I don't!) with **2 tablespoons olive oil**, the lemon zest, **1 teaspoon salt**, and **¼ teaspoon pepper**. Push them to one side—they can be touching, but ideally not overlapping.

3. Place the **halibut** on the empty side of the sheet pan, sprinkle with **salt** and **pepper**, and spread **1 tablespoon pesto** over the top of each fillet.

4. Roast until the green beans are tender and the fish flakes easily, 13 to 15 minutes. If your beans need more time, just transfer the fish to plates and cook the beans for a few more minutes.

5. Halve the zested lemon and squeeze the juice from one half over the fish and green beans. Cut the remaining lemon half into 4 wedges. Serve the halibut and green beans with the lemon wedges alongside for squeezing.

SPICY CHIPOTLE CAULIFLOWER TACOS

1 large head cauliflower
1 medium red onion
Kosher salt
1 chipotle pepper (from a can of chipotles in adobo), plus 2 teaspoons adobo sauce (see Tip)
1 bunch cilantro, leaves and tender stems only
2 limes
1 large ripe avocado
3 tablespoons neutral oil, plus more as needed
1 teaspoon smoked paprika
½ teaspoon ground cumin
12 (6-inch) corn tortillas
2 ounces feta cheese

TIP
The rest of the chipotles and adobo sauce can be frozen for later use—just transfer to an airtight container (or portion into a few small zip-top bags) and freeze for up to 4 months.

SHORTCUT
If you don't feel like cutting up a whole head of cauliflower, buy 3 pounds of precut florets.

BULK IT UP
I don't believe in sides on taco night (just eat more tacos!), but if you must—the Crisp Greens with Lemon Vinaigrette (page 249) would make a great side salad. If you REALLY must, the one-pot rice and beans on page 112 would also be excellent.

SERVES 4

East of Texas is a really fun BBQ restaurant in my hometown, Winston-Salem, North Carolina, that has tons of outdoor space for the kids to run around, plus gigantic margaritas—two of my top criteria for a good time. Whenever it's on the specials board, I get their smoked cauliflower. It's perfectly tender, smoky, and full of flavor. Even my meat-loving husband adores it, so I re-created it at home using ingredients like chipotles in adobo sauce and smoked paprika since cooking in a smoker isn't always in the cards.

1. Slice the **cauliflower** into 1-inch slabs, then roughly chop. Dice the **onion**. Place the cauliflower (including all the little pieces that fall off!) and onion in your largest skillet.

2. Add ⅓ **cup water** and **2 teaspoons salt** to the skillet, cover, and cook over medium heat for about 8 minutes, until the cauliflower is slightly softened but not yet tender, uncovering to stir halfway through.

3. Meanwhile, dice the **chipotle** (if you don't like spice, also remove the seeds) and chop enough **cilantro** to fill ½ cup. Halve **1 lime**.

4. Dice the **avocado**. In a small bowl, combine the avocado, the juice from the halved lime, 2 tablespoons of the cilantro, and a **big pinch of salt**. Mash to combine well.

5. Uncover the cauliflower, increase the heat to medium-high, and stir until any excess water has evaporated, a minute or two. Add the **oil** and cook, stirring often, until the cauliflower has browned a bit, 3 to 5 minutes. Stir in the diced chipotle plus the **adobo sauce**, **paprika**, and **cumin**. Cook, stirring occasionally, until the cauliflower is dark golden brown, 3 to 5 minutes more. If the skillet begins to look dry, add a bit more oil. Remove from the heat, then stir in ¼ cup of the cilantro.

6. If you have a gas stove, turn a few burners to medium heat, place the **tortillas** directly on top of the open flames, and cook until just charred, 15 to 20 seconds per side. If you don't have a gas stove, warm the tortillas in a skillet over medium-high heat, working in batches as needed.

7. Layer the tortillas with mashed avocado and cauliflower, crumble some **feta** on top, and finish with more cilantro. Cut the remaining **lime** into wedges and serve them alongside for squeezing.

LEMONY GARLIC BUTTER SHRIMP ORZO

4 garlic cloves
1 lemon
1½ pounds large (16 to 20
    count) shrimp, peeled and
    deveined
Extra-virgin olive oil
Kosher salt
1 large shallot
2 tablespoons unsalted butter
½ teaspoon red pepper flakes,
    plus more for serving
3 cups low-sodium chicken
    stock, plus more as needed
1½ cups orzo
1 cup fresh basil leaves, plus
    more for serving
1½ cups fresh or frozen peas
½ cup freshly grated Parmesan
    cheese, plus more for
    serving

TIP
If using fresh peas, add them at the same time you add the shrimp, in an even layer on top.

RIFF
Instead of shrimp, make this recipe with pesto meatballs (see page 122). First, sear the meatballs, then transfer them to a plate. Nestle them into the orzo when the recipe cues you to add the shrimp—they'll finish cooking through during those final 5 minutes.

SERVES 4

Sometimes one-pot meals taste delicious but look like a pot full of beige slop. Sometimes they're both delish *and* look like absolutely gorgeous works of art that you can't help but snap a photo of to post to your feed. This recipe is the latter. Not only does the garlicky, cheesy, lemony orzo and shrimp taste perfect, but it's also a gasp-worthy type of stunning when you set it on the dinner table. Serve this one family style so you can show off your masterpiece!

1. Grate **2 of the garlic cloves** into a large bowl. Zest the **lemon** and add half the zest to the bowl; reserve the rest for garnish and set the zested lemon aside. Add the **shrimp**, **1 tablespoon olive oil**, and **¾ teaspoon salt**. Set aside to marinate at room temperature for at least 10 minutes, or in the refrigerator for up to 12 hours.

2. Mince the **shallot** and remaining **2 garlic cloves**.

3. Melt the **butter** in a 12-inch skillet over medium heat. Add the shallot, garlic, and **red pepper flakes** and cook, stirring often, until softened, about 4 minutes. Stir in the **chicken stock** and the **orzo**, increase the heat to high, and bring to a boil. Reduce the heat to low, cover, and cook until much of the liquid has been absorbed, about 8 minutes.

4. Arrange the marinated shrimp in an even layer on top of the orzo. Cover and cook for about 5 minutes, until most of the shrimp are opaque, pink, and cooked through (but some might still be a bit translucent).

5. While the shrimp cooks, finely chop the **basil**.

6. Stir the **peas** (see Tip), **Parm**, and basil into the shrimp. Halve the zested lemon and squeeze in the juice. Cover and cook until the peas are warm and the Parm melts, 2 to 3 minutes. Add more stock if the skillet is beginning to look dry. The orzo should be a nice risotto-y consistency, but not too thick. Taste and adjust the seasoning.

7. Garnish with more basil, the reserved lemon zest, red pepper flakes, and Parm just before serving family-style.

HOT BUTTERED SHRIMP
with Crunchy Cucumber Avocado Salad

1 English (hothouse) cucumber
1 bunch cilantro
1 lemon
1 lime
1 tablespoon plus 2 teaspoons hot sauce (I like Cholula)
Kosher salt
¼ teaspoon garlic powder
8 to 12 tostadas (depending on appetites)
1 tablespoon extra-virgin olive oil
1½ pounds medium (41 to 50 count) shrimp, peeled and deveined
2 tablespoons unsalted butter
1 large ripe avocado

RIFF Try making the shrimp with Frank's RedHot Buffalo Wing Sauce for hot-wings-meets-shrimp vibes.

SHORTCUT You can skip toasting the tostadas if you're pressed for time, but they are crunchier and tastier when toasted. You can also skip the cucumber avocado salad entirely, and just grab store-bought guac and serve that alongside the shrimp.

SERVES 4

Something kind of magical happens when you combine hot sauce and butter—it's creamy, it's spicy, it's tangy. Add shrimp and you've got a spicy, creamy seafood feast. A crisp and creamy avocado cucumber salad is the perfect partner to balance out the heat. Break up tostadas into big shards and scoop a bit of shrimp and a bit of salad onto every bite.

1. Preheat the oven to 300°F.

2. Dice the **cucumber** and chop the **cilantro** (you should have 1 cup) and combine them in a medium bowl. Cut the **lemon** and **lime** in half and squeeze their juice into the bowl. Add **2 teaspoons of the hot sauce**, **½ teaspoon salt**, and the **garlic powder**. Set aside to marinate.

3. Place the **tostadas** on a baking sheet and warm in the oven for 10 minutes.

4. Meanwhile, warm the **olive oil** in your largest skillet over medium-high heat. When it shimmers, add the **shrimp** in an even layer, sprinkle with salt, and cook, undisturbed, until golden brown on the bottom, 2 to 3 minutes. Flip, season the second side with salt, and cook until opaque, another minute. Turn off the heat and stir in the **butter** and the remaining **1 tablespoon hot sauce** until melted and coating the shrimp, about 1 minute.

5. Just before serving, dice the **avocado**, add to the cucumbers, and gently stir to mix.

6. Divide the shrimp and salad among four bowls and serve with tostadas alongside for scooping everything up and making perfect bites. Extra hot sauce, too!

4 tablespoons (½ stick) unsalted butter

1 cup fresh cilantro leaves and tender stems

½ cup panko breadcrumbs

Kosher salt

1½ pounds cod fillets

1 tablespoon extra-virgin olive oil

2 tablespoons mild harissa, plus more for serving

1½ teaspoons honey

1 large ripe avocado

½ cup sour cream

1 lime

12 to 16 flour or corn tortillas (depending on appetites!)

1 (8- to 10-ounce) bag shredded green cabbage or coleslaw mix

RIFF
Not in the mood for tacos? Switch the harissa for sriracha and serve the fish with peanut noods (page 52) or coconut rice (see page 188).

SWAP
I love the grain-free almond and cashew tortillas that have become popular, not because I avoid grains, but because they're an easy way to add protein to my meals. And I think they taste great! I particularly like Siete brand.

SERVES 4

When we lived in San Diego, we loved trolling the county for the best Baja-style (that is, battered and fried) fish tacos. Deep-fried foods are *not* on the list of things I'm willing to cook when I don't feel like cooking, but topping cod with a buttery panko mixture before baking gives a similar crunchy breaded fish taco vibe, with about a tenth of the effort. No need to drive all over San Diego County when you can make these at home in just 30 minutes!

1. Preheat the oven to 425°F. Line a rimmed baking sheet with parchment paper.

2. Melt the **butter** in a microwave-safe medium bowl in 20-second bursts, stirring after each, or in a skillet over medium heat.

3. Chop the **cilantro**. Stir 2 tablespoons of the cilantro, the **panko**, and a **big pinch of salt** into the melted butter (do this right in the skillet if you used one to melt the butter).

4. On the prepared baking sheet, coat the **cod** with the **olive oil**, **harissa**, **honey**, and **1 teaspoon salt**. Use your hands to spread them evenly over the fish. Firmly press the panko mixture on top of the fish.

5. Roast until the fish is opaque and flakes easily with a fork and the panko is golden brown, 10 to 12 minutes. (If the panko hasn't browned, broil it for a few minutes. Turn the oven light on and sit in front of it and watch the whole time—it'll go from brown to burnt very quickly!)

6. While the fish roasts, in a small bowl, mash together the **avocado**, **sour cream**, and **½ teaspoon salt**. Cut the **lime** in half and squeeze the juice from one half into the bowl, then taste and add more lime juice as desired.

7. If you have a gas stove, turn a few burners to medium heat, place the **tortillas** directly on top of the open flames, and cook until just charred, 15 to 20 seconds per side. If you don't have a gas stove, warm the tortillas in a skillet over medium-high heat, working in batches as needed.

8. Use a fork to flake the fish into pieces. Let your crew build their tacos with fish, a bit of **cabbage**, the remaining cilantro, the avocado-lime sauce, and more harissa if they enjoy spice.

PERFECT-EVERY-TIME SCALLOPS
with Herby Cheese Grits

1½ pounds large fresh sea
    scallops, tough ligament
    removed (see Learn)
Kosher salt and freshly ground
    black pepper
2 teaspoons smoked paprika
1 teaspoon ground cumin
2 cups whole milk, plus more as
    needed
1 cup grits or quick-cooking
    polenta
4 basil sprigs
2 ounces goat cheese
¼ cup freshly grated Parmesan
    cheese
3 tablespoons unsalted butter
Extra-virgin olive oil

RIFF
Sear the scallops as
instructed, then cook a diced
shallot and 2 tablespoons of
capers in the 2 tablespoons
of butter in the skillet (add
more butter if the skillet
looks dry) until the shallot
is soft. Stir in the juice of
1/2 lemon and 2 tablespoons
of finely chopped parsley and
pour it over the scallops.

LEARN
There's a small
rectangular tag of tissue on
the side of scallops. It feels
tougher than the rest of the
scallop and its muscle fibers
run opposite the fibers in the
scallop itself. To remove,
pinch it between your thumb
and pointer finger and tear it
away. Not every scallop will
have one, so just remove it
when obvious.

SERVES 4

Fun fact: Shrimp and grits was invented at an adorable little restaurant called Crook's Corner in Chapel Hill, North Carolina, where I went to college. In fact, my parents met my then-freshman-year-boyfriend, now-husband at Crook's. Needless to say, the dish is near and dear to me, and not just because it's so dang tasty. I love playing around with the combo of seafood + corn product—blackened fish with fresh creamed corn, shrimp and polenta— but these scallops with herby cheese grits are my favorite, and, well, perfect every time.

1. Pat the **scallops** completely dry. Season all over with **1 teaspoon salt, smoked paprika, cumin,** and **several grinds of pepper**.

2. In a medium saucepan, bring the **milk** to a gentle boil over medium-high heat. As soon as you start to see little bubbles, stir in the **grits** and reduce the heat to medium. Cook, stirring often, until the grits are thick, 4 to 5 minutes.

3. Meanwhile, pluck off and finely chop the leaves from the **basil sprigs**.

4. Stir most of the chopped basil into the grits along with the **goat cheese, Parm, 1 tablespoon of the butter, 1 teaspoon salt,** and **several grinds of pepper**. Turn off the heat and cover.

5. Warm a 12-inch skillet (preferably stainless steel or cast iron) over medium-high heat. When you flick a drop of water into it and it dances around the pan, it's hot enough. Pat the scallops dry one more time. Add **2 tablespoons olive oil** and swirl the pan to coat. When the oil shimmers, add the scallops and cook, undisturbed, until golden brown on the bottom, 2 to 3 minutes. Flip, add the remaining **2 tablespoons butter** to the pan, and cook, tilting the pan and scooping the butter up with a spoon and pouring it over the scallops, until the scallops are golden brown on the second side, another 1 to 2 minutes.

6. Uncover the grits and give them a big stir, adding a splash of milk if necessary to loosen them up to a risotto-ish consistency.

7. Place a nice scoop of grits in each of four low bowls or plates and add the scallops and any leftover butter/juices from the skillet on top. Garnish with the remaining basil.

LAMB & HUMMUS BOWLS

4 pita breads
2 tablespoons extra-virgin
olive oil
1 pound ground lamb
1½ teaspoons kosher salt
1 tablespoon harissa
1 teaspoon smoked paprika
1 teaspoon garlic powder
½ teaspoon dried oregano
1 bunch dill
¼ cup toasted pistachios
1 (15-ounce) can diced
tomatoes, with their juices
1 (10-ounce) container hummus

RIFF
Make some rice or any grain and grab your favorite greens (arugula would be great) to make grain bowls.

SWAP
Ground beef or pork would swap nicely for the lamb. Swap in store-bought tzatziki if you don't love hummus.

SERVES 4

In 2017, George and I spent a week in Israel, and it's still in first place for our favorite culinary destination. The food is fresh, bright, and flavorful. I thought I was decently familiar with Israeli and Jewish cuisine, but it wasn't until that trip that I learned hummus isn't just a dip or a condiment—it's also used as a base for so many meals. This version of lamb hummus isn't purely Israeli—it's a hodgepodge of flavors I love—but piling saucy meat on top of hummus and scooping it up with pita is something I learned in the culinary wonderland of Shuk Ha'Carmel, the most incredible food market I've ever visited.

1. Preheat the oven to 300°F. Wrap the **pitas** in aluminum foil and place them in the oven, directly on the rack, while you prepare the rest of the meal (you don't have to wait until the oven hits 300°F to throw them in).

2. Warm the **olive oil** in a large skillet over medium-high heat. Add the **lamb**, **1 teaspoon of the salt**, the **harissa**, **paprika**, **garlic powder**, and **oregano**. Cook, using a wooden spoon to break up the lamb into tiny crumbles, until cooked through and browned all over, 7 to 8 minutes.

3. While the lamb cooks, finely chop the **dill** (fronds and tender stems only). Chop the **pistachios**.

4. Stir ½ cup of the dill, the **tomatoes**, and remaining ½ **teaspoon salt** into the skillet with the lamb. Reduce the heat to medium and cook until the lamb mixture is thickened to about the consistency of a Bolognese, 6 to 7 minutes.

5. Divide the **hummus** among four low bowls and use the back of your spoon to swoop it around the bottom surfaces. Top each with the lamb mixture, dividing it evenly. Sprinkle with the chopped pistachios and lots of dill. Serve with the warmed pitas alongside for scooping.

ONE-POT SQUASH-TA

2 medium yellow summer squash (about 1 pound)

1 fennel bulb

2½ cups low-sodium vegetable stock, plus more as needed

8 ounces orecchiette or other short pasta

5 basil sprigs

1 teaspoon kosher salt, plus more as needed

¼ teaspoon dried oregano

Pinch of red pepper flakes

1 lemon

4 garlic cloves

½ cup freshly grated Parmesan cheese

¼ cup freshly grated Pecorino Romano cheese

LEARN
I love adding toasty breadcrumbs on top of pasta for a little crunch. Melt 3 tablespoons butter in a small skillet, then stir in 1/2 cup breadcrumbs, a pinch of salt, a shake of garlic powder, and a few grinds of pepper. Stir until golden brown, et voilà.

SERVES 4 TO 6

This one-pot pasta was the love child of my proclivity for stockpiling pasta while I was pregnant and the one and only summer that George decided to grow a vegetable garden. Overabundance of pasta, overabundance of squash . . . meet squash-ta. If you have a picky eater to feed, omit the fennel, lemon, and basil for a dish that tastes (and looks!) exactly like mac and cheese, but with a pound of hidden veggies!

1. Dice the **squash**. Thinly slice the **fennel**.

2. In a large pot, combine the squash, fennel, **stock**, **pasta**, **2 basil sprigs**, the **salt**, **oregano**, and the **red pepper flakes**. Use a Microplane to grate the zest from half the **lemon** and the **garlic** directly into the pot; set the zested lemon aside.

3. Bring the stock to a boil over high heat, then reduce the heat to medium-high and cook, stirring often, until the pasta is tender (check the box and cook for a few more minutes than the recommended time for al dente). If the liquid evaporates before the pasta is tender, add another ¼ cup stock and continue cooking.

4. While the pasta cooks, thinly slice the leaves from the remaining **basil sprigs**.

5. Pluck out and discard the basil sprigs. Halve the zested lemon and squeeze the juice into the pot, then stir in both **cheeses** and the sliced basil and cook until a thick, creamy sauce forms, 2 to 3 minutes. If it doesn't look creamy, add another splash of stock or water to loosen it up.

6. Taste and adjust the seasoning as needed. Divide among bowls and enjoy.

FIRST DATE SHRIMP SKILLET

1 medium red onion
3 bell peppers (I like using red, yellow, and orange, but anything works)
2 tablespoons extra-virgin olive oil
4 ears white corn, or 2 cups frozen white corn kernels
4 garlic cloves
1 cup fresh basil leaves
Kosher salt and freshly ground black pepper
1 teaspoon garlic powder
1 teaspoon smoked paprika
¼ teaspoon red pepper flakes
1 pound large (16 to 20 count) shrimp, peeled and deveined
1 lemon
2 tablespoons unsalted butter

RIFF
Creamy Shrimp Skillet: Stir in 3/4 cup half-and-half and 1/4 cup freshly grated Parmesan cheese before the last 3 minutes of cooking.

Pesto Shrimp Skillet: Omit the basil and stir in 1/4 cup pesto. Dollop more on top at the end.

Make It Cheesy: Sometimes I just like to add a bit of feta or goat cheese on top!

BULK IT UP
Serve it over polenta (see page 143), couscous (see page 203), or even coconut rice (see page 188).

SERVES 4

Okay, so it wasn't actually our first date, but the first time I ever cooked for George, in a little house in Chapel Hill on Mint Springs Lane that I lived in with three of my girlfriends, I made him Ina Garten's Confetti Corn with Seared Tuna. We both remember the meal vividly—not particularly because of how perfectly it was cooked (I was nineteen years old and cooking on my sister's hand-me-down college pans, after all), but because of how intimate and special it is to cook for the people you love (especially when you're first falling in love!). We have three kids now, so that recipe has been truncated to this quicker version with shrimp cooked in the same skillet, but we both still get a little bit heart-eyed every time I make it.

1. Thinly slice the **onion** and the **bell peppers**. Meanwhile, warm the **olive oil** in your largest skillet over high heat. When it shimmers, add the onion and peppers and cook, stirring occasionally, until golden brown, 9 to 12 minutes.

2. Meanwhile, if using fresh **corn**, slice the kernels off the cobs. Mince the **garlic**. Thinly slice enough **basil leaves** to pack ½ cup.

3. Reduce the heat to medium and stir in the corn, garlic, **2 teaspoons salt**, the **garlic powder**, **paprika**, and **red pepper flakes**. Cook, stirring occasionally, until the spices are fragrant, 2 to 3 minutes more.

4. Place the shrimp on top of the vegetables in an even layer and season with **salt** and **black pepper**. Cover the skillet and cook until the shrimp are pink and opaque, 2 to 4 minutes.

5. Stir in most of the basil. Halve the **lemon** and squeeze in the juice, then add the **butter**. When the butter is melted, remove from the heat and serve, with the remaining basil on top.

CABBAGE-IO E PEPE

1¾ teaspoons kosher salt, plus more for seasoning
1 pound spaghetti
1 head green cabbage
3 tablespoons extra-virgin olive oil
1½ teaspoons freshly ground black pepper
1½ cups freshly grated Parmesan cheese, plus more for serving
1 lemon

SWAP
Instead of cabbage, try swapping in shredded Brussels sprouts, or thinly sliced kale or Swiss chard. If you use Brussels, it's really nice with orecchiette pasta.

SHORTCUT
Grab two 10-ounce bags of shredded cabbage so that you don't have to cut it yourself.

Use a blender to grate your fresh Parm! Cut it into a few big hunks, throw it in, and blend on high speed until it's a fine powder, 10 to 20 seconds.

LEARN
When you inevitably forget to reserve some pasta water, you can make a starchy substitute by stirring 1/4 teaspoon cornstarch into every 1 cup water.

SERVES 4 TO 6

Have I mentioned I'm obsessed with cabbage? (Yes, yes I have.) If you've never had cacio e pepe, it's a simple, classic Italian pasta that literally translates to "cheese and pepper." It's creamy, with a bite from all the black pepper. One night I was making cacio e pepe when I remembered I had leftover caramelized cabbage in the fridge. I thought, *What if . . .* , threw it into the pot, and the next thing you knew, we were slurping down Cabbage-io e Pepe and losing our minds. It's become one of our favorite "there's nothing to eat!" meals because we *always* have spaghetti, cabbage, and Parm in the house.

1. Bring a large pot of salted water to a boil over high heat. Add the **spaghetti** and cook until al dente according to the package instructions. Scoop out at least **2 cups of the pasta cooking water** and set it aside. DO NOT FORGET TO DO THIS! Drain the pasta, then return it to the pot.

2. While the pasta cooks, halve the **cabbage**, remove and discard the core, and thinly slice the cabbage.

3. In a large skillet, warm the **olive oil** and **pepper** over medium-high heat until sizzling and fragrant, about 3 minutes. Add the cabbage and **1 teaspoon of the salt**. Cook, using tongs to toss occasionally, until tender and browned, 7 to 10 minutes. Remove the skillet from the heat.

4. To the pot with the drained pasta, add 1 cup of the reserved pasta cooking water, **½ cup of the Parm** (sprinkle it all over; don't dump it in a pile), and the remaining **¼ teaspoon salt**. Cut the **lemon** in half and squeeze in the juice. Use the tongs to stir and toss vigorously (!!!) until all the cheese is melted, about 2 minutes. Add another **½ cup of the Parm** and, if needed, more pasta cooking water, and toss-stir until a glossy sauce forms, another 2 minutes. Add the remaining **½ cup Parm** and keep stirring in more pasta cooking water as needed until the sauce is even glossier, 2 minutes. If the cheese isn't melting nicely, you can turn the stove heat back to medium-low to warm it up. The noodles should be lightly coated all over; they should not be dry.

5. Toss the cabbage into the pasta. Divide the pasta among bowls, being sure to get lots of cabbage in each serving. Serve with more Parm and tuck right in.

QUICKIE VEGGIE CHILI

1 medium white onion
1 red bell pepper
1 zucchini
1 jalapeño
4 garlic cloves
2 tablespoons extra-virgin
  olive oil
Kosher salt
2 teaspoons ground cumin
1½ teaspoons dried oregano
1 teaspoon smoked paprika
1 (28-ounce) can fire-roasted
  diced tomatoes
1 (15-ounce) cans black beans,
  drained and rinsed
1 (15-ounce) can white beans,
  such as navy, cannellini, or
  butter beans, drained and
  rinsed
Toppings (optional): cilantro,
  sour cream, avocado, hot
  sauce, shredded cheese

SERVES 4

A cup of chili topped with a dollop of sour cream and a sprinkle of cheese is my personal brand of comfort. Warm spices, hearty ingredients, decadent toppings . . . how could that not boost your mood? Most chilis are cooked low and slow for hours, but this one is designed to be quick and efficient yet still taste like it's been labored over. I don't reserve chili for the chilly months—you'll find some variation of this quickie version on my stovetop or in my refrigerator all year round.

1. Chop the **onion**, **bell pepper**, and **zucchini**. Seed (if desired) and mince the **jalapeño**. Mince the **garlic**.

2. Warm the **olive oil** in a wide heavy-bottomed pot over medium-high heat. When it shimmers, add the onion, bell pepper, zucchini, jalapeño, and garlic. Season with **1½ teaspoons salt**, then cook, stirring often, until the vegetables have softened, 6 to 7 minutes. Add the **cumin**, **oregano**, and **paprika** and cook until fragrant, another minute.

3. Add the **tomatoes**, **black beans**, and **white beans** and season with a **big pinch of salt**. Stir to combine, then bring to a very gentle boil. When it begins bubbling, reduce the heat to medium-low and simmer until the tomatoes soften, about 20 minutes. Taste and adjust the seasonings as needed.

4. Serve with whatever **toppings** you like.

LEARN
When you want a soup or chili to cook quickly, do it in your widest skillet or pot. More surface area allows more steam (aka moisture) to escape, which helps the dish thicken and develop flavor much more quickly.

RIFF
Make a chorizo veggie chili by adding 1/2 pound ground chorizo while the veggies cook.

Make a chili cornbread skillet by mixing up a cornbread box mix, pouring it over the finished chili, and baking at 425°F for 20 to 25 minutes.

SHORTCUT
Instead of chopping veggies by hand, throw everything in the food processor. Be sure to do one veggie at a time—doing them all at once will lead to big uneven pieces.

LEMON PANCAKES

1 cup cottage cheese
2 large eggs
1¾ cups whole milk
2 tablespoons maple syrup, plus more for serving
1 tablespoon neutral oil
2 teaspoons pure vanilla extract
1 lemon
2 cups all-purpose flour
2¼ teaspoons baking powder
½ teaspoon baking soda
1 teaspoon kosher salt
4 tablespoons (½ stick) unsalted butter, plus more for serving

TIP
I believe pancakes are an "eat 'em as they come" kind of meal, but if you want everyone to eat together, you can throw them on a baking sheet in a 200°F oven to keep them warm as you cook.

This recipe makes a really big batch on purpose-if you're going to the effort, you should make extra, let them cool, then freeze them in a big zip-top bag for future you.

SWAP
Try ricotta in place of the cottage cheese, and/or 1 teaspoon orange zest instead of lemon zest.

SHORTCUT
If you can find whipped cottage cheese, buy that instead and bypass the cottage-cheese-smashing step.

MAKES ABOUT 17 (3-INCH) PANCAKES

Pancakes for dinner! Here's a version my family devours, and it's loaded with protein from the cottage cheese to keep everyone full for way longer than your standard carb-bomb stack. If cottage cheese freaks you out, try to look past that for this recipe—I promise you cannot taste it or see it once the pancakes are cooked. We're going to use my favorite trick to avoid dirtying up a second bowl: Just dump all the dry ingredients right on top of the wet ones, then use your fingers to sift everything together.

1. Warm your largest nonstick skillet over medium heat so it'll be ready to rock by the time you've finished making the batter.

2. Place the **cottage cheese** in a large bowl and use a fork to smash the curds into even smaller bits as much as possible. Stir in the **eggs**, **milk**, **maple syrup**, **oil**, and **vanilla**. Grate the zest from the **lemon** directly into the bowl, then stir to combine well.

3. In this order, dump the **flour**, **baking powder**, **baking soda**, and **salt** all right on top of each other into the bowl, then use your (clean) fingers to sift the dry ingredients together. Stir the dry ingredients into the wet ingredients. Don't overmix; some lumps are okay. Let the mixture rest for about 5 minutes.

4. Melt **1 tablespoon of the butter** in the skillet and swirl the pan to coat well. Working in batches, add the batter to the pan in as big or small portions as you like 'em—I usually use a ¼-cup measuring cup to make 3-ish-inch pancakes. Cook until golden brown on the bottom and the bubbles on top begin to pop, about 3 minutes. Use a spatula to flip and cook until golden brown on the second side, 2 to 3 minutes more. Repeat until all the pancakes are cooked, adding more butter to the skillet as needed when it looks dry.

5. Serve with extra butter and maple syrup.

HELLA GREEN PASTA

Kosher salt
1 large bunch lacinato kale
  (about 12 ounces)
6 garlic cloves, peeled
1 pound any shape dried pasta
2 lemons
⅓ cup extra-virgin olive oil
1 cup freshly grated Parmesan
  cheese, plus more for
  serving
¼ teaspoon red pepper flakes,
  plus more for serving

LEARN
Boiling the garlic tempers its fiery bite, making it smoother and more mellow.

Typically when you're cooking with kale, you want to remove the tough, fibrous stems for easier eating, but here there's no need! Boiling softens them enough that they blend up smoothly.

SWAP
Instead of kale, try spinach or Swiss chard. They'll taste relatively similar in the end, with all that added garlic and Parm!

SERVES 4 TO 6

Want to trick a bunch of people into eating a pound of kale? Look no further. This bright green pasta has been rebranded "green monster pasta" in my home, and it's one of my very favorite ways to get my children to eat leafy greens. Kids or not, this pasta tastes bright from the lemon and creamy from blending it with starchy cooking water, Parm, and extra-virgin olive oil. Even when you make it for yourself, you won't believe you're eating a pasta sauce made from kale.

1. Bring a large pot of salted water to a boil over high heat. Add the **kale** and **garlic** to the boiling water and cook until the kale is very limp and the garlic is fork-tender, about 8 minutes. Use tongs to transfer the kale and garlic to a blender (do not drain the pot!), squeezing out excess moisture from the kale before you add it to the blender.

2. Return the pot of water to a boil over high heat. Add the **pasta** and cook to al dente according to the package instructions. Scoop out **1 cup of the pasta cooking water**, then drain the pasta and return it to the pot.

3. While the pasta cooks, grate the zest from **1 lemon** directly into the blender. Cut the zested lemon and the **unzested lemon** in half and squeeze their juice into the blender. Add the **olive oil**, **Parm**, **1 teaspoon salt**, and the **red pepper flakes**. Blend on high speed until smooth, adding pasta cooking water a splash at a time as needed to achieve a thick sauce. Don't burn out your blender—just add more water if needed to get it to move. Taste and adjust the seasonings as desired.

4. Pour the sauce over the pasta (you don't have to use it *all*, but I love pasta super saucy, so I do!) and toss to coat well. Add a bit more of the reserved pasta cooking water if needed to achieve a saucy consistency; it shouldn't be too thick, but it should be glossy and stick to the noodles.

5. Divide the pasta among bowls and garnish with more Parm and red pepper flakes before serving.

CHEESY RICE & BEANS

2½ cups low-sodium vegetable or chicken stock

1 (12-ounce) jar red or green salsa (mild or spicy, depending on preference)

1½ cups long-grain white rice

1 (14-ounce) can black or pinto beans, drained and rinsed

2 tablespoons tomato paste

1 teaspoon garlic powder

¼ teaspoon red pepper flakes

¼ teaspoon kosher salt, plus more as needed

1 cup shredded Mexican cheese blend or cheddar cheese

Toppings (optional): thinly sliced avocado, pickled jalapeños, chopped fresh cilantro, sour cream

SERVES 4 TO 6

An inflation-proof meal that stands the test of time? Rice and beans! When I was broke and living in New York City in my early twenties, rice and beans were a staple. My girlfriends and I would all gather in one of our preposterously tiny apartments after working our preposterously underpaid jobs to cook dinner together. Rice and beans with all the toppings was one of our repeat meals. This was before the days of Venmo, so to make things even, we would each pick up one or two ingredients at a bodega before meeting up. Back then we cooked our rice and beans in separate pots because we didn't yet have a million kids and hadn't yet begun loathing dirty dishes as much as we do now as busy moms. But I swear, cooking the rice and beans together in the same pot makes this meal not only even easier, but also more delicious. Don't skimp on the toppings!

1. In a large heavy-bottomed pot or skillet, combine the **stock**, **salsa**, **rice**, **beans**, **tomato paste**, **garlic powder**, **red pepper flakes**, and **salt**. Place over high heat and bring to a boil. Stir to mix well, then reduce the heat to low. Cover and cook until the liquid is absorbed and the rice is tender, 20 minutes.

2. Uncover, turn off the heat, and give it another big stir—don't worry if it's a little stuck to the bottom! Taste and add more salt as needed.

3. Sprinkle the **cheese** over the top, cover, and let stand for 10 minutes, until the cheese is melted.

4. Serve directly from the pot and let people add whatever **toppings** they like!

LEARN
You can throw the whole pot under the broiler if you want to brown the cheese (as long as you cooked it in something oven-safe).

RIFF
Make burritos! Instead of adding cheese on top, place a few tablespoons of cheese down the center of a burrito-size tortilla, load it with the rice and beans, and roll it up.

BULK IT UP
Cook 1/2 pound ground beef or chorizo over medium-high heat. Season it with a big pinch of salt and 1 tablespoon taco seasoning. No need to drain the fat before adding in the rest of the ingredients and proceeding with the recipe as written.

THAI VEGGIE CHOP

1½ cups roasted salted cashew
  pieces
1 bunch cilantro
2 large romaine hearts
Kosher salt and freshly ground
  black pepper
1 large ripe avocado
2½ cups shelled edamame
1½ cups shredded carrots
1 cup wonton strips or chow
  mein noodles
1 tablespoon red curry paste
1 tablespoon sesame oil
1 tablespoon low-sodium soy
  sauce
3 tablespoons rice wine vinegar
1 tablespoon honey

TIP
I highly recommend
doubling the curry cashew
dressing—it'll keep in
your fridge in an airtight
container for up to 1 week, or
you can freeze it!

RIFF
Make it a Thai Chicken
Chop by adding 2 cups shredded
rotisserie chicken, or a
Crispy Tofu Chop by adding
Crispy Miso Lime Tofu
(page 60).

SERVES 4 TO 6

This salad does it all. You get tons of protein from the cashews and edamame, making this a fantastic plant-based lunch or dinner option. The creamy, sorta-spicy, nutty, herby salad dressing will be become your next obsession. Pro tip: I highly recommend chopping this one into itty bitty tiny pieces so you can eat this salad with a soup spoon. It gets more into your mouth faster and will quickly become the way that you want to eat all your salads.

1. Place ½ **cup of the cashews** into a blender and cover with warm water. Set aside to soak.

2. Meanwhile, grab a really large serving bowl. Chop the **cilantro** and **romaine**. Reserve ½ cup cilantro and throw the rest into the bowl along with all the romaine. Season with a **big pinch each of salt** and **pepper**. Dice the **avocado** and toss it into the bowl along with the **edamame**, **carrots**, remaining **1 cup cashews**, and the **wonton strips**.

3. Now finish making the dressing. Drain the liquid out of the blender and add the reserved cilantro, the **red curry paste**, **sesame oil**, **soy sauce**, **vinegar**, **honey**, a **pinch of salt**, and ⅓ **cup water**. Blend on high speed until smooth, about 30 seconds. If it's too thick, blend in more water, 1 tablespoon at a time, until it reaches your desired consistency.

4. Add ⅓ cup of the dressing to the salad and toss to coat well. Add more dressing as desired. Chop the salad (yes, again!) into tiny pieces. Divide among four bowls and chow down!

LEMON PARM CRISPY WHITE BEAN & ARTICHOKE SALAD

1 (15-ounce) can cannellini or white beans

1 (12-ounce) jar marinated artichoke hearts

4 large slices crusty bread

3 tablespoons plus ¼ cup extra-virgin olive oil

Kosher salt and freshly ground black pepper

1 teaspoon garlic powder

1 teaspoon Italian seasoning

2 bunches curly kale

2 cups (about 3 ounces) shaved Parmesan cheese (or 1 cup grated)

2 lemons

SWAP
Chickpeas or any white bean will be wonderful in place of cannellini.

BULK IT UP
Make it a chicken salad by adding 1 1/2 pounds boneless, skinless chicken thighs to the baking sheet from the start, and just add a little bit more of the oil and seasonings to coat them nicely. Chop it up before tossing into the salad.

SERVES 4

One of my greatest achievements in twelve years of marriage has been converting my husband to Team Salad for Dinner. Tucking into a gigantic bowl of greens, preferably with tons of toppings and crunchy things and cheese, is one of my favorite feel-good ways to end the day. If George is going to be convinced to eat salad (especially a—gasp—vegetarian salad) for dinner, it has to be full of the good stuff—crispy warm vegetables, garlicky croutons, lots of cheese, and a tangy no-fuss dressing.

1. Preheat the oven to 400°F. Line a rimmed baking sheet with parchment paper.

2. Drain and rinse the **cannellini beans** in a large colander, then pour the **artichoke hearts** directly over the beans and toss them together so the artichoke juices coat the beans a bit. Pour the beans and artichokes onto the prepared baking sheet and pat them completely dry. Cut the **bread** into cubes and add it to the sheet. Drizzle on **3 tablespoons of the olive oil** and sprinkle with **1¼ teaspoons salt**, **several grinds of pepper**, the **garlic powder**, and **Italian seasoning**. Toss to coat well, then spread everything into an even layer.

3. Bake for 15 to 20 minutes, until the beans and croutons are crispy. (You can remove the croutons and continue cooking the beans and artichokes to get them even crispier, if desired. I do this if I have time, but it's great either way.)

4. Meanwhile, stem and finely chop the **kale** leaves. Place the kale in a large serving bowl and season with a **big pinch each of salt** and **pepper**. Using your hands, massage (aka squeeze) the kale about 7 times, until tender.

5. Add the crispy white beans and croutons, **Parm**, and remaining **¼ cup olive oil**. Juice both **lemons** over the top and toss to coat. Taste and add more salt and pepper as needed.

6. Divide the salad among four low bowls and enjoy immediately.

TURKEY TACO SALAD

FOR THE TURKEY

1 tablespoon extra-virgin olive oil

1 pound ground turkey

2 cups fresh or frozen corn kernels (from 4 ears of corn)

1 (15-ounce) can black beans, drained and rinsed

1 tablespoon chili powder

1½ teaspoons kosher salt

1 teaspoon ground cumin

1 teaspoon smoked paprika

1 teaspoon garlic powder

1 lime

FOR THE SALAD

2 romaine hearts

1 bunch cilantro

¼ cup salsa verde

¼ cup extra-virgin olive oil

3 tablespoons sour cream, plus more for serving

Kosher salt

1 (10- to 14-ounce) bag coleslaw mix

8 ounces shredded white cheddar cheese

2 cups tortilla chips, for serving

Hot sauce, for serving (optional)

SERVES 4

Several years ago, I started a salad club with three of my friends in Carmel Valley. Once a week, we meet at one of our houses for a quick hangout and, well, a salad. This turkey taco salad is one of my repeat recipes when it's my turn to host: It's got lean protein and plant protein, so much flavor and texture, and it's simple to throw together but always impresses.

1. **Make the turkey:** Warm the **olive oil** in your largest skillet over medium-high heat. When it shimmers, add the **ground turkey**. Cook, using a wooden spoon to break it up, until the meat is cooked through and no liquid remains in the skillet, 5 to 7 minutes. Reduce the heat to medium-low and add the **corn**, **beans**, **chili powder**, **salt**, **cumin**, **paprika**, and **garlic powder**. Juice the **lime** into the skillet and cook, stirring occasionally, until the mixture has thickened and is no longer liquidy, 3 to 5 minutes.

2. **Make the salad:** Thinly slice the **romaine** and finely chop the **cilantro**.

3. In a large bowl, whisk together the **salsa verde**, **olive oil**, **sour cream**, and a **pinch of salt**. Add the romaine, cilantro, and **coleslaw** and season with another **big pinch of salt**. Add the **cheddar** and the turkey mixture and toss to mix well.

4. Divide the salad among bowls and crumble lots of **tortilla chips** over the top just before serving. I also like to add a few shakes of **hot sauce** and an extra dollop of sour cream.

RIFF
Not in the mood for a salad? Use the turkey, corn, and bean mixture to make tacos, quesadillas, or a fajita filling instead.

SWAP
Use any ground meat. Veggies like diced zucchini or bell peppers will be great in place of the corn and black beans. Oh, and you will not be disappointed if you swap in Cool Ranch Doritos for the tortilla chips.

SHORTCUT
I love using taco seasoning to speed things up when I'm cooking Mexican food. Instead of measuring out all the individual spices listed, just add 2 tablespoons of taco seasoning.

45 MINUTES

PESTO MEATBALLS
with Tomato Salad & Labneh

FOR THE PESTO MEATBALLS

1 pound 90/10 ground beef
1 large egg
⅓ cup panko breadcrumbs
2 tablespoons pesto
½ teaspoon kosher salt
¼ teaspoon freshly ground
     black pepper
1 tablespoon extra-virgin olive
     oil

FOR THE TOMATO SALAD

3 tablespoons pesto
1 lemon
Kosher salt and freshly ground
     black pepper
1 pound of the best tomatoes
     you can find (cherry,
     heirloom, Roma, etc.)
1 English (hothouse) cucumber
1 large ripe avocado
1 small red onion

TO SERVE

4 slices of good sourdough
     bread, or 4 pitas
Extra-virgin olive oil, for
     drizzling
1 cup labneh or sour cream

SERVES 4

The trick to making really good meatballs with very few ingredients is to use a light touch when forming the meatballs—don't smoosh the meat together. Pesto makes quick work of dinnertime by doubling as the key flavor in the meatballs and as an herby dressing for the salad.

1. **Make the meatballs:** In a large bowl, use your hands to ever so gently combine the **ground beef**, **egg**, **panko**, **pesto**, **salt**, and **pepper**. Lightly roll the mixture into 12 meatballs. Don't pack the meat too tightly or they'll be dense.

2. Warm the **olive oil** in a large nonstick skillet over medium-high heat. When it shimmers, add the meatballs and cook until crisped up and cooked through, shaking the pan to turn them every minute or so, 8 to 10 minutes total. Transfer the meatballs to a plate and wipe out the skillet.

3. **Meanwhile, make the tomato salad:** In a large serving bowl, stir together the **pesto**, the juice of the **lemon**, and a **big pinch each of salt** and **pepper**. Chop the **tomatoes** into bite-size pieces. Peel the **cucumber** like a zebra (see Learn), then cut it into ¼-inch-thick half-moons. Dice the **avocado**. Thinly slice the **onion**. Add all the vegetables to the bowl with the dressing and toss to coat well.

4. Drizzle the **bread** with a **bit of olive oil** and toast in the skillet over medium-high heat until golden brown all over, about 3 minutes per side.

5. Swoop the **labneh** over the bottom of four plates or shallow bowls, dividing it evenly. Add a big scoop of the tomato salad and 3 meatballs to each plate. Serve with the bread alongside for dipping and scooping.

LEARN
Peeling your cucumber like a zebra means this: Peel every other strip off so that it looks striped like a zebra when you're finished with it. This allows the cucumber to hold its shape without getting mushy, but makes it more enjoyable to chew. I also use this technique when cooking with eggplant.

RIFF
Make it on a sheet pan with broccoli: throw the meatballs and 1 pound of broccoli florets tossed in EVOO, salt, and pepper onto a rimmed baking sheet and roast on 400°F for 15 minutes. Swoop some more pesto on the plate and pile the meatballs and broccoli on top. Garnish with some crunchy toasted nuts if you've got 'em!

BULK IT UP
Serve over couscous or rice instead of bread or pita if you'd rather have more of a grain bowl.

CHEESY BEEF & SWEET POTATO FLAUTAS

1 pound sweet potatoes
1 pound 80/20 ground beef
1¾ teaspoons kosher salt, plus
 more as needed
1½ teaspoons ground cumin
1½ teaspoons chili powder
1 teaspoon smoked paprika
1 teaspoon garlic powder
½ teaspoon onion powder
12 (8-inch) flour tortillas
1 cup shredded sharp cheddar
 cheese
Nonstick cooking spray
½ head iceberg lettuce
1 cup sour cream
1 teaspoon lime juice or any
 clear vinegar

RIFF Practically any leftovers can become flautas! Chop up leftover meat and/ or veg, throw some cheese in there, roll it up, and bake.

SWAP Don't love sweet potatoes made savory? Use russets here instead.

MAKES 12 FLAUTAS

I love sweet potatoes cooked in savory ways. Here, we shred them and cook them with ground beef and lots of warm spices to create a tender, super-flavorful flauta filling. Flautas are traditionally fried, but we aren't busting out the deep fryer with this recipe; we're simply spraying them with some cooking oil and baking until the shell becomes shatteringly crisp. I always make some sort of dip—mashed avocado, or a creamy dip made from yogurt or sour cream—and that's the entire meal.

1. Preheat the oven to 400°F. Line a rimmed baking sheet with parchment paper.

2. Peel the **sweet potatoes** and grate them on the largest holes of a box grater.

3. In a large skillet over medium-high heat, cook the **ground beef**, using a wooden spoon or spatula to break it up into tiny crumbles, until a bit of fat renders and collects in the skillet, about 3 minutes. Add the shredded sweet potatoes, **salt, 1 teaspoon of the cumin, 1 teaspoon of the chili powder**, the **paprika**, **garlic powder**, and **onion powder**. Cook, stirring often, until the beef is cooked through and the sweet potatoes are tender, 4 to 5 minutes more. Stir in **2 tablespoons water** during the final minute.

4. Meanwhile, stack the **tortillas** and warm them in the microwave for a few seconds until flexible. Fill each tortilla down the center with the beef mixture, then sprinkle on the **cheese**, dividing it evenly. Roll them up tightly and place them seam side down on the prepared baking sheet.

5. Coat the flautas with **cooking spray**, then bake for 15 to 20 minutes, until crispy and browned.

6. Meanwhile, thinly slice the **lettuce**. In a medium bowl, stir together the **sour cream**, **lime juice**, the remaining ½ **teaspoon cumin**, the remaining ½ **teaspoon chili powder**, and a **pinch of salt**. Taste and adjust the seasoning as needed.

7. Serve the flautas with the sliced lettuce piled on top, dolloped with the creamy chili sauce. Eat the whole mess with a fork and knife.

GRILLED FLANK STEAK
with Charred Corn Panzanella

2 tablespoons brown sugar
2 teaspoons smoked paprika
2 teaspoons garlic powder
2 teaspoons onion powder
Kosher salt and freshly ground
    black pepper
1 (1½- to 2-pound) flank steak
1 pound tomatoes
8 ounces ciliegine mozzarella
    balls
½ small red onion
1 cup fresh basil leaves
3 tablespoons extra-virgin
    olive oil, plus more as needed
2 tablespoons red wine vinegar,
    plus more as needed
1 teaspoon honey
4 ears corn (preferably white),
    shucked
4 (½-inch-thick) slices
    sourdough bread

TIP
No grill? Cook the steak over medium-high heat in a large skillet for 4 to 5 minutes per side. Roast the corn in the oven by brushing it with oil, placing it on a baking sheet, and roasting on 425°F for 10 minutes.

LEARN
Lay the corn down on its side to easily slice off the kernels without them flying all over the place.

SWAP
Swap in roasted butternut squash, eggplant, or crispy white beans (see page 172) for the corn and tomatoes, to continue making this dish year-round.

SERVES 4 TO 6

One bite of this meal, and I am instantly transported to summer nights, eating dinner way past bedtime around my backyard pool in Winston-Salem, North Carolina. My mom and dad make an excellent cook-and-griller team—Mom in the kitchen whipping up magical marinades; Dad manning the flames outside. We've cooked so many variations of this meal over the years, but at its core there's always grilled meat, grilled bread, and a slew of veggies with a delicious, zippy dressing.

1. On a large plate, combine the **brown sugar**, **paprika**, **garlic powder**, **onion powder**, **2 teaspoons salt**, and **½ teaspoon pepper**. Stir to mix well. Pat the **steak** dry, then drag it through the rub, using your hands to spread it evenly and make it stick. Let marinate at room temperature for at least 15 minutes, or uncovered in the refrigerator for up to 24 hours. (Leaving the steak uncovered will allow it to dry out—in a good way—which will help you achieve those great grill marks!)

2. Heat an outdoor grill to medium-high (400° to 450°F).

3. Meanwhile, halve the **tomatoes** (or slice into wedges if large) and **mozzarella** and slice the **onion** and **basil**.

4. In a large serving bowl, whisk together the **olive oil**, **vinegar**, **honey**, **1½ teaspoons salt**, and **a few grinds of pepper**. Add the onions and smush them down to submerge them. Add the mozzarella and basil, then place the tomatoes on top. Do not mix yet! If you do, the tomatoes will absorb the salt and release too much liquid.

5. Lightly coat the marinated steak, **corn**, and **bread** with **olive oil**.

6. Grill the corn and steaks with the lid closed for about 5 minutes, until the corn is charred and the steak is golden brown. Flip the steak, rotate the corn, and cook on the second side for 4 to 5 minutes more, or until an instant-read thermometer inserted into the steak registers 130°F for medium-rare, 140°F for medium, or 150°F for medium-well and the corn is charred all over. Transfer the steak and corn to a serving platter.

7. Grill the bread with the grill open until golden brown grill marks appear, a minute or two. Watch them closely—bread loves to catch on fire when left unattended!

8. When the corn and bread are cool enough to handle, slice the kernels off the cobs and cut the bread into small cubes. Add both to the serving bowl. Toss to combine everything well, then taste and add more salt (you'll likely want a lot more!), olive oil, and vinegar as needed. Serve!

SAUSAGE & PEPPER FRITTATA

½ pound mild or hot Italian
  sausages, casings removed
1 red bell pepper, thinly sliced
Huge handful of baby kale
Kosher salt
8 large eggs
⅓ cup whole milk or heavy
  cream
¾ teaspoon garlic powder
¼ teaspoon red pepper flakes
1½ cups shredded cheddar
  cheese
⅓ cup finely chopped fresh
  basil

TIP
Don't have the right skillet? After sautéing the peppers and sausage, transfer them to a greased 10-ish-inch baking dish (cake pan! Pyrex! whatever!) and gently stir in the egg mixture. Proceed as written.

LEARN
If you use a cast-iron pan instead of a nonstick, the dish will cook faster, so be sure to check the frittata on the lower end of the time range.

RIFF
Make a puff pastry quiche instead. Unroll a thawed sheet of puff pastry into the bottom of a separate 10-inch skillet or pie dish and crimp it over the edges to form a rustic crust. Pour in the filling (sausage, peppers, eggs, and all), cover with foil, and bake at 350°F for 40 minutes, then remove the foil and bake for 10 minutes more. Let cool before slicing.

SERVES 4 TO 6

One of my silver linings of the 2020–2021 lockdown era was teaching hundreds and hundreds of Zoom cooking classes—everything from charity events to private birthday parties and corporate team-building events. One of my menu options was a brunch—starting with strawberry mimosas, then making biscuits and this slow-cooked frittata. Frittatas are a fabulous breakfast, lunch, or dinner, and cooking them over low heat makes the eggs so soft and tender. This sausage-pepper-kale combo is equal parts hearty and nutritious, but check out page 131 to see how to cook up your own frittata creations.

1. Preheat the oven to 250°F.

2. In a 10-inch nonstick ovenproof skillet, combine the **sausage** and **bell pepper** over medium-high heat. Cook, stirring, until the sausage is cooked through and the pepper is tender, 4 to 5 minutes. Add the **baby kale**, tearing it into smaller pieces as you toss it into the skillet, season with a **big pinch of salt**, and cook until wilted, about 2 minutes. Remove from the heat.

3. Meanwhile, in a large bowl, whisk together the **eggs**, **milk**, **¼ teaspoon salt**, the **garlic powder**, and the **red pepper flakes**. Stir in the **cheese** and **basil**. Pour the egg mixture into the skillet. Be sure the sausage and peppers are evenly distributed around the pan.

4. Bake for 20 to 30 minutes, until the center is no longer wobbly. Let it rest for 4 minutes, then use a spatula to loosen the frittata from the skillet and slide it onto a cutting board. Slice into 4 to 6 triangles and serve.

FRITTATA
how you
WANT-TA

2 CUPS OF "ADD-INS"
6 LARGE EGGS
¼ CUP WHOLE MILK OR HEAVY CREAM
YOUR PREFERRED SPICES/SEASONINGS
+ 1 CUP SHREDDED CHEESE

THIS IS MY FORMULA FOR MAKING A FRITTATA USING ANYTHING YOU HAVE HANDY. IT'S THE ULTIMATE CLEAN-OUT-THE-FRIDGE MEAL.

If the "add-ins" aren't something you'd eat raw, cook them in a little oil in a 10-inch ovenproof nonstick skillet until tender. In a bowl, whisk together the eggs, milk, your preferred spices, and 1 cup cheese, then pour the mixture into the skillet.

For extra-tender egg, I prefer to cook frittatas at 250°F for 20 to 30 minutes, until the center is no longer wobbly. But if you're strapped for time, bake it in a 400°F oven for 15 to 20 minutes.

To make it dairy-free, I love using cashew or almond yogurt instead of milk or cream.

A few ideas:

BROCCOLI CHEDDAR FRITTATA
2 cups finely chopped broccoli + 1 minced shallot + 1/4 teaspoon garlic powder + 1/4 teaspoon onion powder + sharp cheddar cheese

MUSHROOM & BRIE FRITTATA
8 ounces sliced mushrooms + 1/4 teaspoon thyme + 1/4 cup freshly grated Parmesan + 2 ounces cubed Brie

PESTO VEGGIE
1 bunch asparagus, 1-inch pieces + 2 thinly sliced scallions + 1/2 cup mozzarella + 1/2 cup feta + spoonfuls of pesto dolloped over top

BACON & BOK CHOY
4 slices chopped bacon + 2 heads thinly sliced baby bok choy + 1 tablespoon sesame seeds + 2 tablespoons gochujang whisked into the eggs + white cheddar

GRILLED PORK CHOPS & ASPARAGUS
with Creamy Pesto

⅓ cup plus 3 tablespoons extra-
   virgin olive oil, plus more for
   grilling
¼ cup apple cider vinegar
1 tablespoon Dijon mustard
Kosher salt and freshly ground
   black pepper
4 garlic cloves
4 (1-inch-thick) bone-in pork
   chops
1 cup fresh soft herbs, such as
   basil, parsley, cilantro, or a
   mix, plus more for serving
½ cup sour cream
⅓ cup roasted almonds,
   walnuts, cashews, pecans,
   or pistachios, plus more for
   serving
1 lemon
2 pounds asparagus
4 ciabatta rolls

TIP
No grill? Cook the pork
chops in a cast-iron skillet
over medium-high heat for 4 to
5 minutes per side. Toss the
asparagus on a rimmed baking
sheet with oil, salt, and
pepper and roast it in a 425°F
oven for 10 to 12 minutes,
until crisp-tender.

SWAP
This simple but
impactful marinade is
wonderful on pork, chicken, or
firm fish.

Any creamy white dairy (or
nondairy) product-yogurt,
ricotta, cottage cheese, etc.-
will work in place of the sour
cream.

SERVES 4

One of my first catering gigs was cooking a private birthday dinner party and I vastly underestimated the amount of olive oil I would need. I didn't have enough to make the pesto that was already embossed on their fancy menu cards, so I used the enormous tub of sour cream that I happened to have in its place. "Creamy pesto!" I exclaimed. They loved it, and it became a staple Cucina Coronado offering. It'll become a staple in your home, too.

1. In a large bowl or zip-top bag, combine **⅓ cup of the olive oil**, the **vinegar**, **mustard**, **1 teaspoon salt**, and **½ teaspoon pepper**. Grate **3 of the garlic cloves** into the bowl. Add the **pork chops**, turn to coat, and let marinate at room temperature for at least 10 minutes or in the refrigerator for up to 48 hours.

2. Prepare an outdoor grill for indirect-heat cooking: If you have a gas grill, turn half the burners on full blast, and turn the others on the lowest heat. If using charcoal, pile the coals to one side of the grill (this will make that side very hot and leave the other side cool).

3. Meanwhile, in a blender or food processor, combine the **herbs**, **sour cream**, **nuts**, **2 tablespoons of the olive oil**, the remaining **garlic clove**, and **½ teaspoon salt**. Cut the **lemon** in half and squeeze the juice from one half into the blender (reserve the other half for the asparagus). Blend until smooth. Taste and add more salt or pepper to the pesto as needed.

4. Trim the bottom 1½ inches from the **asparagus**. On a serving platter, toss the asparagus with the remaining **1 tablespoon olive oil** and a **big pinch each of salt** and **pepper**.

5. Remove the pork chops from the marinade and place them on a plate. Pat dry with paper towels. Rub with a little **olive oil**. Cook the pork chops on the hot side of the grill until dark grill marks emerge, 3 to 4 minutes per side. Move them to indirect heat, add the **ciabatta rolls** to the indirect heat as well, and cook until an instant-read thermometer inserted into the pork registers 145°F and the rolls are light golden, another minute or two. Transfer both to a plate and tent with foil to keep warm.

6. Place the asparagus on the hot side of the grill. Cook, using tongs to keep moving them around, until they're charred all over and feel tender but not squishy, 4 to 5 minutes. Return them to the platter and squeeze the juice from the remaining lemon half over the top.

7. Serve the pork chops and asparagus with a big scoop of the creamy pesto.

ONE-PAN AL PASTOR ENCHILADAS

MAKES 6 ENCHILADAS

I am a big sweet-and-savory lover, so I've always adored tacos al pastor, in which pork is marinated in pineapple juice and a variety of spices, then spit-roasted. I don't exactly feel like breaking out the spit roaster on a Wednesday night, but I *do* crave these flavors often, so I came up with these easy al pastor–inspired enchiladas using ground pork and a can of crushed pineapple.

FOR THE FILLING

1 pound ground pork
1 teaspoon garlic powder
1 teaspoon chili powder
1 teaspoon ground cumin
1 teaspoon dried oregano
1 teaspoon kosher salt
1 (5-ounce) bag fresh spinach
1 (16-ounce) jar salsa verde
½ cup crushed pineapple (from a can, or minced fresh)

TO ASSEMBLE AND SERVE

6 (10-inch) flour tortillas (see Swap)
2 cups shredded pepper Jack cheese
Toppings (optional): pickled red onion, avocado, cilantro, scallions, hot sauce, sour cream

TIP Buy the runny salsa verde in a jar from the shelf-stable section (not the thick refrigerated kind).

SWAP You can also make this dish with ten 6-inch corn tortillas. Wrap them in slightly damp paper towels and microwave for 20 to 40 seconds until warm and pliable, then use about 1/4 cup filling in each.

SHORTCUT Make tacos: Call it quits after cooking the enchilada filling; simply fill up tortillas with the pork and pineapple mixture and a sprinkle of cheese or some sliced avocado.

1. Preheat the oven to 400°F.

2. **Make the filling:** Warm a 12-inch ovenproof skillet over medium-high heat. Add the **pork** to the pan and cook, using a wooden spoon to break it up into tiny crumbles, until barely any pink remains, about 4 minutes. Stir in the **garlic powder**, **chili powder**, **cumin**, **oregano**, and **salt** and cook, stirring, until the pork is cooked through, an additional minute or two. Stir in the **spinach**, tearing it as you add it, **¼ cup of the salsa verde** (reserve the rest of the jar for assembling the enchiladas), and the **pineapple** and cook until the meat has absorbed the sauce, 1 to 2 minutes. Turn off the heat.

3. **Assemble the enchiladas:** Lay the **tortillas** on a clean surface. Spoon about ½ cup of the pork mixture down the center of each tortilla. Top each with about **2 tablespoons of the cheese**. Roll up tightly and line up the enchiladas, seam side down, on a cutting board.

4. When all of the meat has been rolled into tortillas, pour **½ cup of the salsa verde** into the skillet you used for the filling (no need to wipe it out first) and spread it to coat the bottom. Add the enchiladas, seam side down. (I can usually fit five across, then wedge one more in along the top.) Pour the remaining **salsa verde** over the enchiladas, then top with the remaining **cheese**. Bake for 15 minutes, or until the cheese is totally melted.

5. Add toppings, if you like—pickled onion, avocado, cilantro, scallions, and so on. Dig in!

THREE THINGS TO DO WITH A PACK OF KING'S HAWAIIAN ROLLS

King's Hawaiian rolls are one of consumer packaged goods' greatest gifts to mankind. I *love* them. I love making simple sandwiches out of them for my kids, I love using them in more elaborate creations, I love dumping butter and minced garlic on top and baking them into sweet and savory dinner rolls. They are magic.

CHICKEN PARM
SLIDERS
(PAGE 140)

HAM, BRIE, & FIG TOASTIES
(PAGE 139)

CRUNCHY SHEET
PAN SLIDERS
(PAGE 138)

CRUNCHY SHEET PAN SLIDERS

1 pound ground beef
   (preferably 90/10)
1 teaspoon kosher salt, plus
   more as needed
¾ teaspoon garlic powder
½ teaspoon freshly ground
   black pepper
½ cup mayonnaise
¼ cup sweet relish or finely
   chopped pickles
3 tablespoons ketchup
1 tablespoon yellow mustard
1 (12-pack) King's Hawaiian
   Original rolls
8 slices Monterey Jack or
   American cheese
2 cups plain kettle-cooked
   potato chips (such as
   Kettle Brand)

RIFF
You can also use this recipe to make delicious regular burgers! Just form the meat into four patties and cook them in a skillet over medium-high heat for 4 to 5 minutes per side, adding the cheese over the patties when you flip them. Use regular-size burger buns.

SHORTCUT
Use 3/4 pound sliced roast beef instead of cooking a burger patty.

MAKES 12 SLIDERS
Sliders made from a gigantic burger patty! In-N-Out–inspired burger sauce! Chips crumbled over the top layer for crunch! I have served these at more get-togethers than I can count—they always disappear within minutes, and people absolutely lose their minds over them.

1. Preheat the oven to 375°F. Line a rimmed baking sheet with parchment paper.

2. On the prepared baking sheet, combine the **beef**, **salt**, **garlic powder**, and **pepper** and use your hands to mix well. Smoosh the beef down into a large rectangle shape, slightly larger than the 12-pack of rolls. Bake the burger patty until firm to the touch, about 12 minutes.

3. Meanwhile, in a small bowl, stir together the **mayo**, **relish**, **ketchup**, **mustard**, and a **pinch of salt** to make the burger sauce.

4. Using a serrated knife, slice the **rolls** crosswise, leaving them all connected, to make one giant top and bottom. Work slowly to make the top and bottom as even in thickness as possible.

5. Place the bottom bun sheet on a piece of parchment paper. Smear the cut side with all the burger sauce. Arrange **4 slices of the cheese** in an even layer over the sauce, tearing them to fit as needed.

6. Remove the cooked burger patty from the oven (but leave the oven on). Use paper towels to pat off excess grease, then place the patty on top of the cheese layer. Discard the parchment paper from the baking sheet and wipe the sheet out. Top the patty with the **remaining 4 slices cheese**, then crumble the **chips** over the top, and close the sandwich with the top bun sheet.

7. Use the parchment paper to pick up the mega-slider and transfer it to the baking sheet.

8. Cover with foil and bake for 10 minutes, then uncover and bake for 2 minutes more, until the cheese is melted and the tops of the buns are light golden brown. Let the sliders rest for a few minutes, then slice them apart and serve.

HAM, BRIE & FIG TOASTIES

1 (12-pack) King's Hawaiian Original rolls
2 tablespoons mayonnaise
1 tablespoon Dijon mustard
3 tablespoons fig jam
½ pound thinly sliced honey-glazed ham
8 ounces Brie
2 tablespoons unsalted butter, melted
1 tablespoon everything bagel seasoning

TIP
If you aren't heating these, you might enjoy adding a layer of arugula to the sandwiches—and you'll want to skip the butter and seasoning on top.

LEARN
I don't take the rind off of Brie when I eat it, but I do ensure that it's room temperature when serving so it tastes the most delicious! Cold Brie (any cold cheese, really) lacks flavor. Remember to take your cheeses out of the fridge 20 to 30 minutes before you want to serve up a cheese board.

SWAP
Pretty much any cold cut, jam, and cheese is delicious. I truly think I've tried every combination imaginable. Turkey, pepper jelly, and sharp white cheddar. Deli-roasted chicken, raspberry jam, and goat cheese. It's hard to go wrong!

MAKES 12 SLIDERS
Show up to a picnic or potluck with these and prepare to be the most popular person at the party. Whether you serve them hot or cold, the sweet and savory elements combine into the tastiest treat of a tiny sandwich.

1. Preheat the oven to 375°F.

2. Using a serrated knife, slice the **rolls** crosswise, leaving them all connected, to make one giant top and bottom. Work slowly to make the top and bottom as even in thickness as possible.

3. Spread the **mayo** and **mustard** over the bottom bun. Spread the **jam** over the top bun.

4. Layer the **ham** over the bottom rolls, then slice the **Brie** (to the best of your ability—it's sticky!) and layer that over the ham. Close the sandwich with the top bun sheet.

5. Brush the **butter** over the top of the rolls. Shake the **everything bagel seasoning** over the top.

6. Tent loosely with foil and bake for 10 minutes, then remove the foil and bake for 2 minutes more, or until the cheese is melty. Let the sliders rest for a few minutes, then slice them apart and serve immediately.

CHICKEN PARM SLIDERS

1 pound ground chicken
1 large egg
½ cup plus 2 tablespoons
   freshly grated Parmesan
   cheese
¼ cup panko breadcrumbs
¼ cup finely chopped fresh
   basil
1 teaspoon garlic powder
Kosher salt and freshly
   ground black pepper
1 (12-pack) King's Hawaiian
   Original rolls
1 cup (4 ounces) shredded
   mozzarella cheese
½ cup marinara sauce, plus
   more for serving
Nonstick cooking spray

RIFF You can use this
meat mixture to make burgers
or meatballs! For burgers,
shape 4 patties and cook
for 5 minutes per side
in an oiled skillet. For
meatballs, roll out 10 of
them and bake at 425°F for
15 minutes.

Speed things up by shredding
3 cups rotisserie chicken
meat and using that instead
of making the chicken patty.
Toss it in a bowl with
everything except the egg
and panko, then load it onto
the rolls and proceed with
the recipe as written.

MAKES 12 SLIDERS

Any time there's a meatball sub on a menu, my husband, George, can't help but order it. And without fail, four bites in, his shirt is covered in red sauce, the sandwich is falling apart in his hands, and he's cursing himself for once again falling prey to the allure of the meatball sub. Enter: the chicken Parm slider. The meatball sub's tidier, cuter, more manageable little sister.

1. Preheat the oven to 400°F. Line a rimmed baking sheet with parchment paper.

2. In a large bowl, combine the **chicken**, **egg**, **½ cup of the Parm**, the **panko**, **basil**, **garlic powder**, **1¼ teaspoons salt**, and **several grinds of pepper** and use your hands to mix well.

3. Place the meat on the prepared baking sheet and smoosh it down into a large rectangle shape, slightly larger than the 12-pack of rolls.

4. Bake for about 15 minutes, until the patty is cooked through (press your finger down on it, it should be firm). It will look FUNKY—lots of liquid will ooze out. Don't worry, that's normal!

5. Using a serrated knife, slice the **rolls** crosswise, leaving them all connected, to make one giant top and bottom. Work slowly to make the top and bottom as even in thickness as possible.

6. Place the bottom bun sheet on a piece of parchment paper and sprinkle with **½ cup of the mozzarella**.

7. Remove the cooked burger patty from the oven (but leave the oven on). Use paper towels to pat off excess grease, then place the patty on top of the mozzarella layer. Discard the parchment paper from the baking sheet and wipe the sheet out. Spread the **marinara sauce** over the patty, top with the remaining **½ cup mozzarella**, and close the sandwich with the top bun sheet.

8. Use the parchment paper to pick up the mega-slider and transfer it to the baking sheet.

9. Coat the top with **cooking spray** and sprinkle with the remaining **2 tablespoons Parm**.

10. Cover with foil and bake for 10 minutes, then uncover and bake for 2 minutes more, until the cheese is melted and the tops of the buns are light golden brown. Let the sliders rest for a few minutes, then slice them apart and serve immediately, with extra marinara for dipping.

PORK CHOPS
with Plums & Polenta

FOR THE PORK CHOPS

4 (1½-inch-thick) boneless pork chops
Kosher salt and freshly ground black pepper
1 tablespoon extra-virgin olive oil

FOR THE POLENTA

2 cups whole milk, plus more as needed
1 cup quick-cooking polenta or grits
⅓ cup freshly grated Parmesan cheese
1 tablespoon fresh thyme leaves
1 tablespoon unsalted butter
Kosher salt and freshly ground black pepper

FOR THE PLUMS

4 large plums
1 large red onion
1 tablespoon extra-virgin olive oil
1 tablespoon fresh thyme leaves
Kosher salt and freshly ground black pepper
2 tablespoons unsalted butter
½ lemon

SWAP
Any stone fruit or apple is great in place of the plums. Apricots, peaches, cherries, Honeycrisp, Granny Smith—they're all wonderful here. Just keep an eye on them, as each fruit will take a slightly different amount of time to soften.

SERVES 4

When we first moved to California, in stereotypical new-to-California fashion, I became completely obsessed with farmers' markets. I'd bop all over San Diego to chase down my favorite vendors. One of the biggest revelations I had was how freaking delicious plums are. Plums come in a variety of shapes and colors! Plums get crossbred with apricots and create *pluots!* I started eating and cooking with them obsessively, and this gorgeous dish is the outcome of that infatuation.

1. **Make the pork chops:** Season the **pork chops** generously with **salt** and **pepper**.

2. Warm the **olive oil** in a 12-inch cast-iron skillet over medium-high heat. Turn on your oven vent—things are about to get smoky! When the oil shimmers, add the pork chops and cook until a golden brown crust forms all over and an instant-read thermometer inserted into the thickest part registers 135°F, 3 to 5 minutes per side. If the edges look pink, use tongs to hold the chops with the edge against the pan and sear for 30 seconds. Transfer the pork chops to a plate and set the pan aside (no need to wipe it out).

3. **Make the polenta:** Warm the **milk** in a medium pot over medium-high heat. When the milk begins to bubble, whisk in the **polenta** and cook, whisking often, until the polenta is soft and thick, about 5 minutes. Turn off the heat and stir in the **Parm**, **thyme**, **butter**, **¾ teaspoon salt**, and **several grinds of pepper**. If it gets too thick, just stir in a bit more milk to loosen it up. Taste and add more salt as needed.

4. **Make the plums:** Slice the **plums** into ¼-inch-thick wedges and pit them. Cut the **onion** into ¼-inch-thick slices. Warm the **olive oil** in the skillet you used for the pork chops over medium heat. When it shimmers, add the onion and **thyme**. Season with a **big pinch each of salt** and **pepper**. Cook, stirring often, until the onions are softened, about 5 minutes. Add the sliced plums and cook, stirring often, until they are soft and warm but not mushy, 3 to 4 minutes. Remove from the heat, stir in the **butter**, and juice the **lemon half** into the plums, stirring to incorporate.

5. Cut the pork chops into ½-inch-thick slices and serve over the polenta, with the plums and onions spooned over the top.

PANKO HONEY MUSTARD CHICKEN
with Frico Broccoli

½ cup grainy Dijon mustard
⅓ cup plus 1 tablespoon honey
  or maple syrup
5 tablespoons extra-virgin
  olive oil
1½ teaspoons garlic powder
¼ teaspoon red pepper flakes
Kosher salt
4 (6- to 8-ounce) boneless,
  skinless chicken breasts
4 tablespoons (½ stick)
  unsalted butter
¾ cup panko breadcrumbs
½ cup freshly grated Parmesan
  cheese
1 pound broccoli florets

SWAP
Use finely chopped almonds or hazelnuts instead of breadcrumbs for a gluten-free spin. Swap in asparagus or green beans for the broccoli.

SHORTCUT
Use store-bought honey mustard instead of making your own.

SERVES 4

Plain ol' boneless, skinless chicken breasts are given new life in this sheet pan meal. The chicken gets coated in a honey mustard sauce, then topped with buttery breadcrumbs that get crunchy and browned in the oven. My kids love this dish—we call it giant chicken nuggets (feeding kids is all about the marketing, amiright?). The broccoli gets the frico treatment—crisped up with Parm. Then dunk everything in the extra honey mustard sauce—that's what it's there for.

1. Preheat the oven to 425°F. Line a baking sheet with parchment paper.

2. In a large bowl, stir together the **mustard**, **honey**, **3 tablespoons of the olive oil**, **1 teaspoon of the garlic powder**, the **red pepper flakes**, and **1 teaspoon salt**. Reserve 3 tablespoons of the sauce in a serving bowl.

3. Add another **½ teaspoon salt** to the sauce in the large bowl, then add the **chicken** and turn to coat evenly. If you have time, let the chicken marinate at room temperature for up to 30 minutes or up to overnight in the refrigerator. But don't worry if you need to cook it right away!

4. Melt the **butter** in a microwave-safe medium bowl in 20-second bursts, stirring after each, or in a skillet over medium heat. Stir in the **panko**, **¼ cup of the Parmesan**, the remaining **½ teaspoon garlic powder**, and a **big pinch of salt** (do this right in the skillet if you used one to melt the butter).

5. On the prepared baking sheet, toss the **broccoli** florets with the remaining **2 tablespoons olive oil** and **¼ teaspoon salt** to coat evenly. Nestle the chicken breasts among the florets. Top with the panko mixture, pressing firmly to adhere.

6. Roast for 12 minutes, then gently toss the broccoli and sprinkle the remaining **¼ cup Parmesan** on top. Roast until an instant-read thermometer inserted into the thickest part of the chicken registers 160°F, 5 to 7 minutes more.

7. Serve the chicken and broccoli with the reserved honey mustard sauce alongside for dunking.

COCONUT CURRY CHICKEN MEATBALLS & VEGGIES

1 red bell pepper
1 bunch cilantro
1 pound ground chicken or
    turkey
⅓ cup panko breadcrumbs
1 large egg
3 tablespoons red curry paste
Kosher salt
2 tablespoons neutral oil
1 (13.5-ounce) can full-fat
    coconut milk
½ cup low-sodium chicken
    stock
2 tablespoons low-sodium soy
    sauce
1 tablespoon fish sauce
1 lime
3 cups baby spinach

SHORTCUT
Grab some frozen store-bought Italian meatballs. Throw them in the skillet when you add the coconut milk. Trust me—it works even though we're mishmashing Italian and Thai flavors.

BULK IT UP
Two ideas: 1) Add a can of drained chickpeas or lentils when you add the coconut milk, or 2) serve the meatballs and veggies over rice or rice noodles.

SERVES 4

A lot of people think they don't like curry, but what they really don't like is curry powder, which is typically a blend of turmeric, cumin, ginger, and black pepper. Curry paste is a totally different ball game—it's made from chiles, garlic, lemongrass, turmeric, and often some shrimp paste for savory umami flavor. Here I use it to create a coconut curry sauce that enrobes chicken meatballs and vegetables for a big skillet of nutritious comfort food.

1. Thinly slice the **bell pepper** and finely chop the **cilantro**.

2. In a large bowl, combine the **chicken**, ⅓ cup of the cilantro, the **panko**, **egg**, **1 tablespoon of the red curry paste**, and **1 teaspoon salt**. Use your hands to mix well, then use a tablespoon (or keep using your hands) to measure and roll 15 to 20 little meatballs.

3. Warm **1 tablespoon of the oil** in a large nonstick skillet over medium-high heat. When it shimmers, add the meatballs and cook until browned all over, 2 to 3 minutes per side. Transfer to a plate.

4. Add the remaining **1 tablespoon oil** to the skillet (no need to wipe it out) and heat over medium-high heat. When it shimmers, add the bell pepper and cook, stirring occasionally, until softened, 3 to 4 minutes. Add the remaining **2 tablespoons red curry paste** and cook, stirring continuously, until it starts to stick, about 30 seconds. Stir in the **coconut milk**, **stock**, **soy sauce**, **fish sauce**, and the juice of the **lime**. Increase the heat to high and bring to a boil, then reduce the heat to medium and cook until the sauce has thickened, 4 to 5 minutes. Gently stir in the meatballs and **spinach**, tearing it with your hands as you add it to the skillet, until the meatballs are coated in curry sauce and the spinach is wilted, 2 to 3 minutes.

5. Divide among bowls and garnish with the remaining cilantro before serving.

WHITE CHICKEN CHILI

3 cups low-sodium chicken stock

2 pounds boneless, skinless chicken thighs

2 (15-ounce) cans white beans, such as cannellini, butter, chickpeas, navy, or great northern, drained and rinsed

1 (16-ounce) jar medium or spicy salsa verde

1 tablespoon ground cumin

2 teaspoons kosher salt, plus more as needed

1 teaspoon dried oregano

1 teaspoon onion powder

1 teaspoon garlic powder

1 teaspoon chili powder

1 bunch curly kale

1 bunch cilantro

2 limes

1 (16-ounce) bag frozen white corn, or the kernels cut from 4 ears fresh corn

⅓ cup heavy cream

1 cup shredded cheddar cheese, plus more for serving

Toppings (optional): your favorite chili accompaniments, such as sour cream, hot sauce, tortilla chips, Fritos, or cornbread

SERVES 6 TO 8

My mom's white chicken (or turkey, if it's the day after Thanksgiving) chili is one of those recipes I can still close my eyes and taste—my memory knows it so well. I picture it bubbling away in her gigantic, banged-up stainless-steel pot on the stove in my childhood home. It's the definition of a simple recipe: There's no stirring, sautéing, or browning necessary. It's flavorful and creamy with juicy chicken and tons of heft. The best part is it's nearly impossible to mess up! Take it from my mom, who set off our fire alarm so often while cooking dinner that she was on a first-name basis with the local firefighters.

1. In a large pot, combine the **stock**, **chicken**, **beans**, **salsa verde**, **cumin**, **salt**, **oregano**, **onion powder**, **garlic powder**, and **chili powder**. Bring to a boil over high heat, then reduce the heat to medium-low, cover, and cook for about 30 minutes, or until the chicken is cooked through.

2. Meanwhile, stem and roughly chop the **kale** leaves. Chop the **cilantro**. Cut **1 lime** in half.

3. Transfer the chicken to a bowl and use two forks to shred it, then return the shredded chicken to the pot. Add the kale, ½ cup of the chopped cilantro, the **corn**, **cream**, **cheese**, and the juice of the halved lime. Cook, uncovered, until the kale is wilted and the chili has thickened, about 5 minutes. Taste and add more salt as needed.

4. Cut the remaining **lime** into wedges. Serve the chili in bowls with the remaining cilantro sprinkled over top, the lime wedges alongside for squeezing, and any other **toppings** or go-withs you like.

SLOW
To make this in a slow cooker, dump in the stock, chicken, beans, salsa verde, cumin, salt, oregano, onion powder, garlic powder, and chili powder, cover, and cook on low for 6 hours. Uncover and stir in the kale, cilantro, cream, cheese, and lime juice and cook with the lid off for 30 minutes more.

SWAP
Add more veggies or switch them around if you want—try diced zucchini or bell pepper, small broccoli or cauliflower florets, and any leafy green such as spinach or chard in place of the kale.

LOWCOUNTRY BOIL
with Old Bay Lemon Butter

½ cup (1 stick) unsalted butter, cut into pieces

4 tablespoons Old Bay seasoning, plus more as needed

1 lemon

3 tablespoons kosher salt, plus more as needed

1 (14- to 16-ounce) kielbasa

4 ears corn, shucked

1 pound little potatoes, such as baby Dutch gold or baby red

3 pounds large (10 to 15 count) shrimp, peeled and deveined

1 small jar cocktail sauce

SWAP
If you're without Old Bay but still want a boil with some kick, make it with hot sauce butter. Instead of Old Bay, swap in equal parts of your fave hot sauce (I like Cholula or sriracha here!).

BULK IT UP
If you can find crab claws, add those when you add the kielbasa and corn.

SERVES 4 TO 6

I grew up spending summers at my grandparents' home on Bald Head Island off the coast of North Carolina. It's the dreamy kind of Southern beach town where the trees drip with Spanish moss, and every stranger waves hello like they're seeing an old friend, so even though the swampy weather makes me a bit batty, I love being there. When we were little, my sister and I used to hitchhike up to the docks and catch shrimp all afternoon, then bring it home for our grandmother Mimi to cook up in a lowcountry boil. We had to peel and de-head our own shrimp after they were boiled, but if you're making this with the convenience of a fishmonger or grocery store, buy them peeled and deveined to make an easy weeknight feast.

1. On a large rimmed baking sheet, scatter around the **butter** and **1 tablespoon of the Old Bay**. Zest the **lemon** over the baking sheet, then cut the zested lemon in half and squeeze the juice over as well.

2. Fill your biggest pot with about 4 quarts water. Add the spent lemon peels, the remaining **3 tablespoons Old Bay**, and the **salt**. Bring to a boil over high heat.

3. While the water boils, cut the **kielbasa** into 1-inch pieces, snap the **corn** in half crosswise, and halve the **potatoes**.

4. When the water is boiling, add the potatoes and cook for 5 minutes. Add the kielbasa and corn and cook until a paring knife easily slides in and out of a potato, 8 minutes more. Finally, add the **shrimp** and cook, stirring gently to ensure they are fully submerged in the hot water, until pink and opaque, 2 to 4 minutes. Drain, then shake the colander to get out all the liquid.

5. Pour the boiled ingredients on the prepared baking sheet. Let them sit to melt the butter, about a minute, then stir everything around to coat well. Sprinkle with more salt and Old Bay.

6. Serve straight from the baking sheet with the **cocktail sauce** alongside for dipping.

SHRIMP, CHEDDAR & CHARRED PINEAPPLE TACOS

4 tablespoons neutral oil
2 tablespoons tomato paste
1 teaspoon smoked paprika
Kosher salt and freshly ground
  black pepper
¾ teaspoon dried oregano
1 tablespoon honey
1 large orange
1 lime
1 cup fresh cilantro
1½ pounds medium (41 to 50
  count) shrimp, peeled and
  deveined
8 to 12 (6-inch) corn tortillas
16 ounces chopped fresh
  pineapple
½ cup shredded white cheddar
  cheese

TIP

Want to make this on the grill? Cut the pineapple into long spears to make it easier to grill and cook for 4 to 5 minutes per side over medium-high heat. Add the shrimp for the last 2 to 3 minutes.

SWAP

Pork would also be delicious with these flavors—plop pork tenderloin in this marinade, then roast it on 425°F with the pineapple for 15 minutes instead of broiling it.

SERVES 4

Taco night at my house is really a do-your-thing meal. George has tacos, I often heat up some frozen brown rice and cut romaine to make myself a burrito bowl, I chop the ingredients up really small for the baby, and I throw everything into a quesadilla for my bigger boys because tacos really befuddle them. All the ingredients for this taco night feast cook on one baking sheet, so I don't mind that every member of my household needs their "taco" prepared differently.

1. In a large bowl, combine **3 tablespoons of the oil**, the **tomato paste**, **paprika**, **1 teaspoon salt**, the **oregano**, **honey**, and **¼ teaspoon pepper**. Juice the **orange** into the bowl. Cut the **lime** in half and squeeze the juice from one half into the bowl; cut the remaining half into 4 wedges and set aside. Chop the **cilantro** and add 1 tablespoon to the bowl. Add the **shrimp** to the marinade and stir to coat. Let marinate at room temperature for at least 20 minutes or in the refrigerator for up to 4 hours.

2. Position racks in the top and bottom thirds of the oven and heat the broiler. Line a rimmed baking sheet with aluminum foil.

3. Stack the **tortillas** on a large piece of aluminum foil and wrap them tightly. Place the packet on the bottom rack of the oven to warm.

4. Meanwhile, on the prepared baking sheet, toss the **pineapple** with the remaining **1 tablespoon oil** and sprinkle with a tiny bit of **salt**. Place the baking sheet on the top rack of the oven and broil for 5 to 7 minutes, until charred in places. Carefully scooch the pineapple to one side of the baking sheet. Remove the shrimp from the marinade, letting the excess drip off, then add them to the baking sheet. (It's okay if they overlap with the pineapple in places.) Broil for an additional 3 to 5 minutes, rotating the baking sheet halfway through, until the shrimp are pink and opaque.

5. Pile the tortillas with your desired amount of **cheese**, shrimp, charred pineapple, and cilantro. Enjoy immediately, with the lime wedges alongside for squeezing.

FANCY FISH

2 lemons
1 large shallot
2 garlic cloves
1 large zucchini
½ pound ripe tomatoes
4 (6-ounce) fish fillets, such as halibut or salmon
4 teaspoons capers, drained
4 tablespoons extra-virgin olive oil
Kosher salt and freshly ground black pepper

SWAP
Any soft, quick-cooking vegetable like green beans, snap or snow peas, broccoli, and so on will work in place of or in addition to the zucchini and tomatoes.

BULK IT UP
This recipe is great on its own, but try adding 1/2 cup frozen rice to the bottom of each packet; it'll steam while the veggies cook.

SERVES 4

Cooking en papillote is one of the fanciest techniques I'm willing to undertake when I don't feel like cooking, but I promise you it is both very easy and very worth the slight extra effort of folding and crimping parchment paper. Essentially, you create little individual steam ovens for your fish and veggies—the parchment packets puff up with steam, allowing the fish and vegetables to cook both quickly and delicately. Magic!

1. Preheat the oven to 350°F.

2. Cut **1 lemon** into 8 thin slices; reserve the other for serving. Thinly slice the **shallot** and **garlic**. Halve the **zucchini** lengthwise and cut into half-moons. Chop the **tomatoes** into 1-inch pieces.

3. Lay out four 15-inch square pieces of parchment paper on a clean surface. Place 2 lemon slices in the center of each. Place the **fish** on top.

4. Divide the chopped vegetables among the pieces of parchment, arranging them along the sides of each fish fillet, along with **1 teaspoon capers** each. Drizzle each packet with **1 tablespoon olive oil** and season generously with **salt** and **pepper**.

5. Working with one packet at a time, gather the edges of the parchment at the top of the fillet and fold it down until you reach the fish, as if you're rolling up a bag of chips. Now fold up each side around the fish and crease tightly so that it holds. It doesn't need to be pretty! Just scrunch it to secure.

6. Place the packets on a rimmed baking sheet and bake for 15 minutes, until the packets are puffed up.

7. Cut the remaining **lemon** into wedges. Carefully open the packets (they'll be steamy!) and serve as is with the lemon wedges alongside.

SRIRACHA SHRIMP SUSHI BOWLS

½ cup plus 1 tablespoon low-
    sodium soy sauce
¼ cup plus 1 tablespoon honey
1 tablespoon sriracha, plus
    more as needed
6 tablespoons rice vinegar
2 pounds large (16 to 20 count)
    shrimp, peeled and deveined
2 cups sushi rice, rinsed
1 English (hothouse) cucumber
½ teaspoon kosher salt
1 large avocado
1 tablespoon toasted sesame
    seeds
Pickled ginger, for serving

RIFF Make teriyaki shrimp bowls by using a store-bought teriyaki marinade/sauce instead of making this sriracha marinade.

SERVES 4 TO 6

I love serving this meal family style—throw the rice, shrimp, cucumbers, avocado, and any other toppings you dig out of the fridge (edamame! shredded carrots! pickled jalapeños!) in the center of the table and let everyone create their own perfect bowl. My kids always eat well on nights when I serve dinner like this, because they love having the authority to build their own meal.

1. In a large bowl, combine **½ cup of the soy sauce**, **¼ cup of the honey**, the **sriracha**, and **3 tablespoons of the vinegar**. Whisk until smooth.

2. Place the **shrimp** in a separate large bowl or zip-top bag. Add about ¼ cup of the marinade and toss to coat. Let marinate at room temperature for at least 20 minutes or in the refrigerator for up to 4 hours. Reserve the remaining marinade for serving.

3. Combine the **rice** and **2½ cups water** in a medium saucepan and bring to a boil over high heat. Reduce the heat to low, cover, and cook for 15 to 17 minutes, until the liquid is absorbed and the rice is tender. Turn off the heat and let stand, still covered, for about 10 minutes more.

4. While the rice cooks, peel the **cucumber** like a zebra (see Learn, page 122), halve it vertically, and scoop out/discard the seedy guts, then thinly slice. Place in a medium bowl. Add the remaining **3 tablespoons vinegar**, remaining **1 tablespoon soy sauce**, remaining **1 tablespoon honey**, and the **salt**. Let marinate at room temperature for at least 10 minutes or in the refrigerator for up to 24 hours. Just before serving, dice the **avocado** and gently toss it with the cucumbers. Sprinkle with the **sesame seeds**.

5. Heat the broiler to high. Line a rimmed baking sheet with aluminum foil.

6. Shake the marinade off the shrimp, then place it in an even layer on the prepared baking sheet and pat completely dry. Broil for 3 to 5 minutes, until pink and opaque.

7. To build bowls, start with a layer of sushi rice, drizzle with some of the reserved marinade, then top with shrimp, marinated cucumbers, and **pickled ginger**. Drizzle with the reserved marinade and more sriracha as desired.

HARISSA ROASTED VEGGIES
with Whipped Feta

1 (15-ounce) can chickpeas
1 pound medium carrots
1 large red onion
3 tablespoons extra-virgin
  olive oil
2 tablespoons harissa, plus
  more for serving
2 teaspoons honey
Kosher salt
1 (8-ounce) block feta cheese
½ cup plain full-fat Greek
  yogurt
½ lemon
Handful of fresh soft herbs,
  such as parsley, dill, cilantro,
  basil, or a mix
Handful of toasted nuts, or
  ¼ cup toasted seeds

RIFF Omit the harissa and honey, and instead toss a big spoonful of pesto into the veggies after they've roasted. Serve with burrata instead of whipped feta.

SHORTCUT Skip the whipped feta and just crumble some feta on top. Find prechopped butternut squash or sweet potatoes at the grocery store and use that instead of carrots.

SERVES 4

Sometimes all I want for dinner is a heap of really well-seasoned roasted vegetables. I chop up whatever veggies need to be used up, throw it all on a sheet pan, make a sauce while it's cooking, and 30 minutes later: dinner. This whipped feta elicits positively indecent responses out of my guests every time I serve it—it's ridiculous.

1. Preheat the oven to 425°F.

2. Dump the **chickpeas** into a colander. Drain them, but do not rinse.

3. Arrange a few layers of paper towels on a rimmed baking sheet, then pour the drained chickpeas on top. Use another paper towel to pat them very dry. Discard all the paper towels, then shake the chickpeas into an even layer. There will be some chickpea skins on the baking sheet now—no need to pick them out. They'll roast up into crispy little bits and be delicious!

4. Cut the **carrots** on the diagonal into ½-inch-thick slabs and thinly slice the **onion**. Add the carrots, onion, **olive oil**, **harissa**, **honey**, and **1 teaspoon salt** to the chickpeas and toss to coat well.

5. Roast for 25 to 30 minutes, until the carrots are golden on the outside but fork-tender.

6. Meanwhile, in a blender or food processor, combine the **feta** and **yogurt**. Zest and juice the **½ lemon** into the blender and add a **pinch of salt**. Blend on high speed until smooth, scraping down the sides as needed, 30 to 45 seconds. If it's too thick and your blender is having a hard time mixing, add a bit of water, a splash at a time, until the desired consistency is achieved.

7. Chop the **herbs** and **nuts**.

8. Taste the roasted veggies and add more salt as needed. Stir in the herbs.

9. Spread a nice spoonful of whipped feta over the bottom of your bowl or plate and top it with a pile of roasted veggies and a sprinkle of nuts. Add another dollop of harissa on top if you love spice.

CRUNCHY REFRIED BEAN TACO-DILLAS
with Lime Crema

1 small yellow onion
3 garlic cloves
2 tablespoons unsalted butter
Kosher salt
¾ teaspoon ground cumin
¾ teaspoon chili powder
2 (15-ounce) cans pinto beans
1 bunch cilantro
10 (8-inch) flour tortillas
1½ cups shredded
   Mexican cheese blend,
   cheddar cheese, or pepper
   Jack cheese
Nonstick cooking spray or
   neutral oil
½ cup sour cream
½ lime

RIFF Use the turkey mixture from the Turkey Taco Salad (page 119) to make crispy turkey tacos, or the pork-and-pineapple filling from the One-Pan al Pastor Enchiladas (page 135) to make crispy al pastor tacos!

Roll these up and cook them like flautas (see page 125).

SHORTCUT I think the beans are worth making, but you can use canned refried beans instead: Warm them up in a pot and add all the seasonings listed before loading them into the tortillas.

SERVES 4

Is it a taco? Is it a quesadilla? It doesn't matter—all that matters is that it's crispy and cheesy and 10,000% delicious. My children will not touch beans on their own, but smashed up with butter and stuffed into a crispy tortilla with cheese? Suddenly, they become bean enthusiasts.

1. Preheat the oven to 425°F. Line a baking sheet with parchment paper.

2. Mince the **onion** and **garlic**. Melt the **butter** in a large skillet over medium heat. Add the onion, garlic, and **1 teaspoon salt** and cook, stirring often, until the onion is soft and translucent, about 5 minutes. Add **½ teaspoon of the cumin** and **½ teaspoon of the chili powder** and cook, stirring frequently, until fragrant, another minute.

3. Open both cans of **pinto beans**. Drain one can, but don't rinse the beans, and add them to the skillet. Dump in the entire second can, including the liquid. Add **4 cilantro sprigs** and **2 tablespoons water**. Bring to a boil over high heat, then reduce the heat to medium and cook, stirring occasionally, until the beans are really thick, resembling gravy, about 10 minutes. Remove from the heat. Pick out and discard the cilantro stems, then use a fork or potato masher to smash the beans. They don't need to be totally smooth, but every bean should be smashed at least a little bit. Taste and add more salt as needed.

4. Place **1 flour tortilla** on the prepared baking sheet and spread about 3 tablespoons of the refried beans all over half of it. Sprinkle **2 to 3 tablespoons of the cheese** over the beans, then fold it closed (you might have to flip it over so the beans are on top to get it to stay folded). Repeat with the remaining tortillas, beans, and cheese, spacing them about 1 inch apart on the baking sheet and using a second parchment-lined baking sheet if needed.

5. Spray the tops with **cooking spray** and bake for 10 to 12 minutes, until the cheese is melted and the tortillas are golden brown.

6. Meanwhile, in a blender, combine the **sour cream**, remaining **cilantro**, the juice of the **½ lime**, remaining **¼ teaspoon cumin**, remaining **¼ teaspoon chili powder**, and a **big pinch of salt**. Blend on high speed until no flecks of cilantro remain, 30 to 45 seconds.

7. Serve the taco-dillas with the crema alongside for dolloping and dipping.

Kosher salt
2 cups brown rice
1 small head cauliflower
   (1 pound)
1 (13.5-ounce) can full-fat
   coconut milk
1 (6-ounce) can or (4-ounce)
   tube tomato paste
2 to 3 tablespoons red curry
   paste
1 tablespoon garam masala
1 teaspoon ground turmeric
   (optional)
1 (15-ounce) can chickpeas
   (don't drain them!)
½ bunch cilantro
3 cups packed fresh spinach
Freshly ground black pepper
Cooked rice, for serving

RIFF
Make a cauliflower coconut curry by omitting the garam masala and adding 1 tablespoon of soy sauce and the juice of 1 lime.

BULK IT UP
If you must have meat, stir in a pound of boneless, skinless chicken breasts cut into 1-inch pieces when you add the cauliflower.

SLOW
To make this in a slow cooker, combine the ingredients from steps 2 and 3 in the slow cooker, cover, and cook on low for 4 hours, then stir in the spinach and cilantro and cook for 20 minutes more to finish.

SERVES 6

This tikki-masala-meets-curry recipe dials up the cozy factor with the creamy coconut milk, the warm spices, and the way the chickpeas and cauliflower absorb the sauce. In Carmel Valley, we are lucky to have gorgeous weather most of the year—but in December and January, it rains and rains and rains. This recipe is on repeat during those chilliest, dampest months.

1. Bring a large pot of salted water to a boil over high heat. Add the **rice** and cook, uncovered, stirring occasionally, until tender, about 30 minutes. Drain and return to the pot. Cover and allow the rice to steam until you're ready to eat.

2. While the rice cooks, chop the **cauliflower** into florets. In a large pot, combine **1¼ cups water**, the **coconut milk**, **tomato paste**, **2 tablespoons of the red curry paste**, the **garam masala**, **2 teaspoons salt**, and the **turmeric** (if using). Place over medium-high heat and whisk to incorporate (the mixture might need to heat up before the ingredients fully combine).

3. When the ingredients are incorporated, stir in the **chickpeas (with their liquid)** and cauliflower. Bring to a boil, then reduce the heat to medium. Cook, stirring occasionally, until the cauliflower and chickpeas are very tender, 20 to 25 minutes. Use a fork to gently smash the chickpeas against the side of the pot—this will naturally thicken the sauce and keep you from biting into a chalky chickpea. Meanwhile, chop the **cilantro**.

4. Stir in the **spinach**, tearing it with your hands as you add it to the pot, and stir to wilt, 2 to 4 minutes. Turn off the heat and stir in most of the cilantro. Taste and add more salt, curry paste, and pepper as needed.

5. Serve the chickpeas over rice, sprinkled with the remaining cilantro.

BRAISED FISH
with Tomato & Coconut Chickpeas

2 (15-ounce) cans chickpeas,
   drained and rinsed
1 (14.5-ounce) can fire-roasted
   diced tomatoes
1 (13.5-ounce) can full-fat
   coconut milk
2 teaspoons ground cumin
2 teaspoons chili powder
1 teaspoon ground turmeric
Kosher salt
2 limes
½ bunch cilantro
2 big handfuls of fresh spinach
4 (6-ounce) cod fillets (or any
   flaky white fish)
Extra-virgin olive oil
Freshly ground black pepper

SERVES 4

Yotam Ottolenghi, an Israeli chef with gorgeous restaurants all over London and the author of some of my favorite cookbooks, has a recipe for Curried Lentil, Tomato, and Coconut Soup that has become a staple in my home during the dreary rainy season that drags on from December through March in Northern California. Those flavors inspired this one-skillet fish. The fish cooks right on top of the stewy spiced chickpeas, giving you a cozy and comforting one-pan meal packed with plant-based and lean protein.

1. In a large skillet, combine the **chickpeas**, **tomatoes**, **coconut milk**, **cumin**, **chili powder**, **turmeric**, and **1½ teaspoons salt**. Cut **1 lime** in half and squeeze the juice into the skillet. Bring to a boil over high heat, then reduce the heat to medium and cook, stirring often, until thickened to the consistency of a stew, 15 to 20 minutes.

2. Chop the **cilantro**. Cut the remaining **lime** into 4 wedges.

3. Lightly smash the chickpeas against the side of the skillet. Stir in the **spinach**, tearing it as you add it, and ¼ cup of the chopped cilantro. Cook until wilted, 2 to 3 minutes.

4. Smoosh the **cod** down into the chickpeas so that the sides are covered but the top is still exposed. Drizzle with a bit of **olive oil** and season with a **big pinch each of salt** and **pepper**. Reduce the heat to low, cover, and simmer, until the fish is opaque and flakes easily with a fork, 6 to 8 minutes.

5. Divide the cod and chickpeas among plates. Scatter the remaining cilantro over the top and serve immediately with the lime wedges for squeezing.

SUMMER SOUP

1 large onion
1 red bell pepper
1 medium zucchini
1 medium yellow squash
4 garlic cloves
¼ cup extra-virgin olive oil, plus
    more for serving
Kosher salt and freshly ground
    black pepper
4 cups low-sodium vegetable
    stock
1 (14.5-ounce) can crushed
    tomatoes
1 (14.5-ounce) can diced
    tomatoes
½ cup Israeli couscous
8 thyme sprigs
2 bay leaves
1½ cups frozen corn (or the
    kernels from 2 ears fresh
    corn)
Freshly grated Parmesan
    cheese, for serving
Lemon wedges, for serving

LEARN
The soup will thicken as it sits—just stir in a splash of water or stock until it's back to the consistency you like.

RIFF
Try swirling a big dollop of pesto into your soup before serving for an herby, cheesy addition.

SWAP
Other vegetables that would be great in here: green beans cut into 1-inch pieces, potatoes, carrots, fennel.

SERVES 4 TO 6

All my Texas cousins are gasping for air just reading the title of this recipe—soup?! In the summer?! If you, too, live on the surface of the sun during the summer months, I completely understand your urge to skip this recipe. But for the rest of us, throwing summer's finest crops—peppers, zucchini, squash, corn, and basil—into a pot and simmering them is a lovely way to make the season's veggies shine and highlight the truest expression of their flavors.

1. Dice the **onion**, **bell pepper**, **zucchini**, and **squash**. Mince the **garlic**. Warm the **olive oil** in a large Dutch oven over medium-high heat. When it shimmers, stir in the onion, bell pepper, zucchini, squash, and garlic and season with **1 teaspoon salt** and **½ teaspoon black pepper**. Cook, stirring occasionally, until the vegetables are softened, 5 to 7 minutes.

2. Add the **stock**, **crushed tomatoes**, **diced tomatoes**, **1 cup water**, the **couscous**, **thyme**, **bay leaves**, and **1 teaspoon salt**. Increase the heat to high and bring to a boil, then reduce the heat to medium-low. Cook, stirring often, until the vegetables are tender, about 8 minutes. Add the **corn** and cook until crisp-tender, 3 minutes more. Taste and add more salt as needed.

3. Ladle the soup into bowls. Drizzle with more olive oil and top with a big sprinkle of **Parm** and some black pepper. Squeeze a **lemon wedge** over the top just before digging in.

TOMATO FARROTTO

1 large shallot

4 garlic cloves

2 tablespoons extra-virgin olive oil

2 pints cherry tomatoes (or any tomatoes, cut into 1-inch pieces)

1 tablespoon fresh oregano leaves

1½ cups pearled farro

3 cups low-sodium vegetable stock, plus more as needed

½ cup fresh parsley leaves and tender stems

½ lemon

¼ cup freshly grated Parmesan cheese, plus more for serving

¾ teaspoon kosher salt, plus more as needed

¼ teaspoon freshly ground black pepper, plus more as needed

SERVES 4 TO 6

I really like farro when it's cooked "correctly"—perfectly chewy, individual grains that can be tossed into a salad or used as a base for a bowl. But I *love* farro when it's (technically) overcooked, simmered until the grains are creamy but still maintain their signature chewiness into a risotto-style dish.

1. Mince the **shallot** and **garlic**. Warm the **olive oil** in a large pot over medium heat. Add the shallot and cook, stirring occasionally, until slightly softened, about 3 minutes. Add the garlic and cook until fragrant, another minute. Add the **tomatoes** and **oregano** and cook, stirring occasionally, until the tomatoes are beginning to burst, 3 to 5 minutes.

2. Stir in the **farro** and **stock**. Increase the heat to high and bring to a boil, then reduce the heat to medium-low. Cook, stirring every few minutes, until the farro is tender and most of the liquid is absorbed, 20 to 30 minutes. Add more stock as needed if the liquid is absorbed before the farro is tender. Meanwhile, finely chop the **parsley**.

3. Reduce the heat to low, juice the **½ lemon** into the pot, and stir in the **Parm**, **salt**, **pepper**, and all but a spoonful of the parsley. Taste and adjust the seasoning as needed. Serve with more Parm and the remaining parsley sprinkled over the top.

TIPS This is a great make-ahead meal; just reheat it with a splash of water or stock.

Check your farro's label and make sure it cooks in under 20 minutes.

SWAP Swap in brown rice or barley for the farro, and try using 2 ounces of goat cheese in place of the Parm for a delightfully tangy farrotto.

BULK IT UP I love farrotto on its own, but it's also fantastic with scallops (page 96) or Cajun salmon (page 74).

SLOW To make this in a slow cooker, throw everything but the lemon juice and Parm into the crock, cover, and cook on low for 4 hours. Remove the lid and stir in the lemon juice and Parm. Cook with the lid off until thickened to your liking (you can turn it up to high to speed this up).

CRISPY WHITE BEAN & CAULIFLOWER TAHINI BOWLS

FOR THE GRAINS

1½ cups of your favorite grain, such as farro, barley, quinoa, or rice

5 parsley sprigs, plus more for serving

1 tablespoon extra-virgin olive oil

1 tablespoon apple cider vinegar

¾ teaspoon kosher salt

FOR THE CAULIFLOWER AND CRISPY WHITE BEANS

1 large head cauliflower

4 tablespoons extra-virgin olive oil

Kosher salt and freshly ground black pepper

1 (15-ounce) can white beans, such as cannellini, butter, chickpeas, navy, or great northern, drained, rinsed, and patted dry

FOR THE TAHINI DRESSING

¼ cup tahini

1 tablespoon harissa

2 teaspoons honey

2 teaspoons low-sodium soy sauce

1 tablespoon apple cider vinegar

¼ teaspoon garlic powder

¼ teaspoon kosher salt

TO SERVE

2 cups arugula (or any greens)

Toasted sesame seeds or any chopped toasted nuts

Finely chopped fresh parsley

LEARN

When cutting the cauliflower on the baking sheet, be careful not to slide your knife along the baking sheet—that will dull it.

SERVES 4

Joseph Leonard, a restaurant in Manhattan's West Village, has been a favorite of mine since I lived above it with several of my girlfriends in my twenties. Now that I live in California and all those girlfriends have left their thimble-size apartments in favor of the suburbs, I don't get my Joseph Leonard fix as often as I'd like. I dream of their tahini cauliflower appetizer, even so many years later, but I finally found a way to re-create it at home and turn it into a main.

1. Preheat the oven to 450°F.

2. **Make the grains:** Cook **your favorite grain** per the package instructions. When the grains are cooked, use kitchen shears to finely snip the **parsley** straight into the pot. Add the **olive oil**, **vinegar**, and **salt**. Remove from the heat and cover to keep warm.

3. **Make the cauliflower and crispy white beans:** Place the **cauliflower** on a rimmed baking sheet. Cut it in half through the stem. Lay the two halves cut side down, then slice them into ½-inch-thick planks. Cut apart the individual florets. There will be little bits of cauliflower everywhere—that's fine! They crisp up wonderfully and are a part of the magic of this recipe. Add **3 tablespoons of the olive oil**, **1 teaspoon salt**, and **a few grinds of pepper**. Toss to coat evenly. Roast for 20 minutes, until the cauliflower has begun to soften. Flip over the cauliflower, then scooch it to one side to make room for the beans.

4. Pour the beans onto the empty space on the baking sheet, drizzle them with the remaining **1 tablespoon olive oil**, and sprinkle with **¼ teaspoon salt** and **a few grinds of pepper**. Spread out the beans and cauliflower so that they are touching as little as possible.

5. Roast for an additional 20 minutes, or until the cauliflower is browned all over and the beans are crispy. If you are looking for even more crispness, heat the broiler to high and place the baking sheet on the bottom rack (yes, bottom!) of the oven for several more minutes. Keep a close eye on it!

6. **Meanwhile, make the tahini dressing:** In a large bowl, whisk together the **tahini**, **1 tablespoon warm water**, the **harissa**, **honey**, **soy sauce**, **vinegar**, **garlic powder**, and **salt**. Add more warm water, a splash at a time, until it's a tiny bit thinner than heavy cream. Add the cauliflower and beans to the bowl and toss to coat.

7. Add a scoop of grains and a handful of **arugula** to each of four bowls. Top with the roasted cauliflower and crispy beans. Garnish with a sprinkle of **sesame seeds** and some **parsley**.

LENTIL BRUSCHETTA
with Pickled Shallot Vinaigrette

1 small shallot

1 lemon

1 tablespoon apple cider vinegar

1 teaspoon honey

½ cup extra-virgin olive oil

4 celery stalks

8 dates

1 cup fresh parsley

2 (14.5-ounce) cans lentils

2 ounces Parmesan cheese

8 slices of good sourdough bread

¼ cup toasted almonds (or any nut you like)

8 ounces ricotta cheese

TIP The bruschetta only gets better as it sits, but I wouldn't push it past 5 days.

SWAP Try using any white bean in place of the lentils, fennel in place of the celery, or whipped feta (see page 159) in place of the ricotta.

BULK IT UP Try mixing in several cups of thinly sliced massaged kale for a big, delicious salad. Just add more EVOO and lemon juice to dress it.

SERVES 4

Some nights, all I really want to eat for dinner is some delicious bread. I. Love. Bread! (Proclaimed in Oprah voice.) White bread with mayo and sliced ripe tomato is unbeatable in the summer, but in the winter months, I love a legume bruschetta like this one. It's salty (Parm!), sweet (dates!), crunchy (celery!), and it's all tied together with a punchy shallot vinaigrette.

1. Mince the **shallot** and transfer it to a large serving bowl. Squeeze the juice from the **lemon** over top and add the **vinegar** and **honey**. Let sit for at least 10 minutes (or cover and refrigerate for up to 24 hours before using). Whisk in ¼ **cup of the olive oil**.

2. Trim and thinly slice the **celery**, then add it to the bowl with the dressing. Remove the pits from the **dates** and chop into small pieces (don't worry if they stick together), then add them to the bowl. Finely chop the **parsley** and throw it into the bowl. Drain and rinse the **lentils**, then add them to the bowl. Use a vegetable peeler to shave the **Parm** directly into the bowl. Toss to combine well and set aside to marinate while you toast the bread.

3. Warm the remaining ¼ **cup olive oil** in a large skillet over medium-high heat. When it shimmers, add the **bread**, working in batches as needed, and cook until golden brown all over, 2 to 3 minutes per side.

4. Meanwhile, chop the **almonds**.

5. Divide the bread among four plates, spread some **ricotta** over each slice, and top with several spoonfuls of the lentil mixture. Sprinkle the chopped almonds over top and enjoy immediately.

TATER TOT EGG BAKE

1 medium yellow onion
1 red bell pepper
2 tablespoons extra-virgin
   olive oil
1 pound frozen tater tots
Kosher salt
8 large eggs
¼ cup whole milk
1 tablespoon hot sauce
1 teaspoon smoked paprika

RIFF
Stir in 1/2 cup chopped Canadian bacon and 1 cup shredded cheddar cheese with the eggs for a nostalgic Denver-omelet-plus-hash-browns situation.

SWAP
To use fresh potatoes instead, grate 1 pound of Yukon Golds on the largest holes of a box grater directly onto a clean kitchen towel. Squeeze out the excess moisture, then cook with the onion and bell pepper as written.

SERVES 6

My friend Jillian worked for Williams-Sonoma corporate for years, and the two of us can gab about food and recipes all day long. She loves cooking beautiful meals for her family, but this potato pancake is what she cooks when she doesn't feel like cooking. Sometimes she just does the tater tots and eggs; sometimes she adds more vegetables and spices, like I do here. I recommend lots of ketchup for the kids, and Obligatory Greens (see pages 248–249) with some prosciutto for the adults. The potato pancake itself is somewhere between a Spanish-style tortilla and a tater tot frittata. Whatever it is, it's delicious.

1. Preheat the oven to 350°F.

2. Thinly slice the **onion** and **bell pepper**.

3. Warm the **olive oil** in a 10-inch ovenproof skillet over medium-high heat. When it shimmers, add the onion, bell pepper, and **tater tots** (the skillet is going to be REALLY full—hang in there) and season with a **big pinch of salt**. Cook, stirring often, until the onion and pepper soften and the tater tots are no longer frozen, 4 to 5 minutes.

4. Meanwhile, in a large bowl, whisk together the **eggs**, **milk**, **hot sauce**, **paprika**, and **1 teaspoon salt**. Pour the egg mixture into the skillet and scooch the tots around to distribute evenly.

5. Transfer the skillet to the oven and bake for 12 to 20 minutes, until the eggs are no longer wobbly in the center.

6. Slide a spatula around the edges of the skillet to dislodge the potato pancake. Slide it onto a plate, cut into 6 pieces, and serve.

1 HOUR

ENCHILADA RICE SKILLET

1 red bell pepper
4 scallions
1 tablespoon neutral oil
1 pound 90/10 ground beef
2 teaspoons chili powder
1½ teaspoons kosher salt
1 teaspoon garlic powder
1 (14.5-ounce) can low-sodium
    beef stock
1 (15-ounce) can black beans,
    drained and rinsed
1 (8- to 10-ounce) jar enchilada
    sauce
1 cup white rice
2 cups shredded cheddar
    cheese
½ cup sour cream
Toppings (optional): thinly
    sliced avocado, pickled
    onions, pickled jalapeños,
    sour cream, thinly sliced
    radishes, hot sauce, cilantro

SWAP
Swap in any veggie you have on hand—broccoli, cauliflower, mushrooms, anything! Any ground meat works, or use an extra can of beans or a plant-based ground meat alternative and use veggie stock to make it a vegetarian meal.

SHORTCUT
Use microwaveable rice to shortcut this recipe: Cook your meat and veggies, then stir in 3 cups of microwaved rice, the enchilada sauce, the black beans, 1 cup of shredded cheese, and the sour cream. Omit the beef stock. Add the remaining cheese on top and broil.

SERVES 4 TO 6

I love a good enchilada night, but sometimes I just want to dump a bunch of stuff in a skillet, throw it in the oven, and call the kids in for dinner 45 minutes later. I love setting out tons of toppings so that everyone can adorn their bowl as they please. This is as close to a casserole as I get, and oh boy is it worth breaking my no-casserole stance.

1. Position a rack in the top of the oven and preheat to 375°F.

2. Dice the **bell pepper** and **scallions**. Set aside 2 tablespoons of the diced scallions.

3. Warm the **oil** in a 12-inch ovenproof skillet over high heat. When it shimmers, add the **ground beef**, bell pepper, remaining scallions, the **chili powder**, **salt**, and **garlic powder**. Cook, using a wooden spoon to break up the beef into tiny crumbles, until almost cooked through, 5 to 7 minutes. Pour off any excess liquid that has collected in the pan.

4. Stir in the **stock**, **beans**, **enchilada sauce**, and **rice**. Bring the mixture to a boil, then cover, transfer the skillet to the oven, and bake, covered, for 45 minutes, or until the rice is tender and all the liquid has been absorbed.

5. Turn the oven to broil. Carefully pull out the skillet and stir in **1 cup of the cheese** and the **sour cream**. Use a spatula to smooth out the top, then sprinkle the remaining **1 cup cheese** over the top.

6. Broil, uncovered, for 2 to 4 minutes, until the cheese is melted, watching it the entire time to make sure it doesn't burn.

7. Garnish with the reserved scallions and any other **toppings** you love before serving.

SHEET PAN SESAME-GINGER STEAK & PEPPERS

⅓ cup extra-virgin olive oil
¼ cup neutral oil
⅓ cup low-sodium soy sauce
⅓ cup rice vinegar
3 tablespoons honey
2 tablespoons tahini
3 garlic cloves
1 (2-inch) piece fresh ginger
Kosher salt
1 (1- to 2-pound) flank steak
3 red, orange, or yellow bell
  peppers
Toasted sesame seeds or
  everything bagel seasoning

TIP This recipe is also great on the grill! Heat your grill to 450°F. Cut each pepper into three big pieces so they won't fall through the grates, then grill until charred all over and slice them after cooking. Grill the steak for about 5 minutes per side, but keep an eye on it with an instant-read thermometer.

SHORTCUT Use a store-bought ginger dressing instead of making this marinade.

BULK IT UP Serve it with sushi rice (see page 206) or heat up some frozen prepared rice.

SERVES 4

I could marinate a shoe in this mixture, and it would still be one of the best things I've ever eaten. It is salty, sweet, and gingery, and it pairs so nicely with flank steak or any other meat or fish (I adore it with halibut). I love a lighter steak meal like this one as a way to enjoy red meat without feeling bogged down afterward.

1. In a blender, combine the **olive oil**, **neutral oil**, **soy sauce**, **vinegar**, **honey**, **tahini**, **garlic**, **ginger** (no need to peel it), and **½ teaspoon salt**. Blend on high speed until smooth, 30 to 45 seconds.

2. Place the **steak** in a resealable plastic bag or large bowl. Add enough marinade just to cover the steak, about ¼ cup. Let marinate at room temperature for at least 30 minutes, or in the refrigerator for up to 48 hours. Cover and refrigerate the remaining marinade (which will become your sauce) until dinnertime.

3. Meanwhile, cut the **bell peppers** into thin strips.

4. Position a rack in the top of the oven and heat the broiler to high. Line a rimmed baking sheet with aluminum foil.

5. Remove the steak from the marinade, letting any excess drip off. Pat it dry and sprinkle with about **1 teaspoon salt**. Place the steak on one side of the prepared baking sheet. Place the peppers on the other side. Add 2 to 3 tablespoons of the marinade and toss to coat well.

6. Broil for 4 minutes, then flip the steak and stir the vegetables. Broil for an additional 4 minutes, until an instant-read thermometer inserted into the steak registers 125° to 130°F for medium-rare. Transfer the steak to a cutting board to rest for at least 5 minutes.

7. Thinly slice the steak against the grain. Arrange on a serving platter along with the broiled peppers. Sprinkle with **sesame seeds** and serve with the remaining marinade alongside.

WHITE CHEDDAR BUTTERMILK BISCUITS & SPICY SAUSAGE GRAVY

1 tablespoon fresh lemon juice

3 cups plus 3 tablespoons
    whole milk

2¼ cups self-rising flour

1 cup shredded sharp white
    cheddar cheese

Kosher salt and freshly ground
    black pepper

½ teaspoon garlic powder

1 large shallot

1 pound hot Italian sausage,
    casings removed

LEARN
If your gravy gets too thick after sitting for a while, just stir in another splash of milk until it's perfect.

RIFF
These biscuits are also, of course, excellent on their own. Scramble some eggs, crisp up some bacon, and serve with butter and jam for a traditional Southern breakfast plate!

SERVES 4 TO 6

This recipe makes my Southern show. Biscuits and gravy are a way of life down South, and when I was growing up, my friends and I loved frequenting the diners around Winston-Salem, North Carolina, ordering big ol' plates of biscuits slopped with beige gravy on top. Traditional biscuits and gravy are delicious, and I honestly feel a little bit nervous messing with such a classic, but I've kicked up the flavor with cheddar and spicy Italian sausage. When I'm feeling homesick, this is the recipe I turn to.

1. Preheat the oven to 475°F. Line a baking sheet with parchment paper.

2. Pour the **lemon juice** into a liquid measuring cup, then pour in **¾ cup plus 3 tablespoons of the milk** so that the combined mixture measures 1 cup. Let sit at room temperature for at least 5 minutes.

3. Meanwhile, in a large bowl, combine **2 cups of the flour**, the **cheese**, **1 teaspoon salt**, the **garlic powder**, and **¼ teaspoon pepper**. Pour in the milk mixture. Use a large wooden spoon to stir until just combined. If a bit of dry flour remains at the bottom of the bowl, use your hands to knead the dough together. Use the spoon to drop 6 biscuits onto the parchment-lined baking sheet, dividing the dough evenly and spacing the biscuits at least 2 inches apart. Flatten them out so they're about 3 inches across.

4. Bake for 8 to 10 minutes, until golden brown on top.

5. Meanwhile, mince the **shallot**.

6. Warm a large skillet over medium-high heat. Add the **sausage** and cook, using a wooden spoon to break up the sausage into small pieces, until almost cooked through, 3 to 4 minutes. Stir in the shallot and cook until the sausage is cooked through and the shallot has softened, 2 to 3 minutes more.

7. Reduce the heat to medium and add the remaining **¼ cup flour**. Cook, stirring, until the flour is pasty and no longer white, about 30 seconds. Slowly pour in the remaining **2¼ cups milk**, stirring continuously and scraping up any bits that are stuck to the bottom of the skillet. Stir in **1¼ teaspoons salt** and **½ teaspoon pepper**. Cook, stirring often, until the gravy thickens enough to coat the back of a spoon, 2 to 3 minutes. Taste and adjust the seasoning as needed.

8. Slice the biscuits in half crosswise and place each biscuit, cut side up, on a plate and smother in gravy. Yum, y'all.

GIANT HAM & CHEESE CROISSANT

4 ounces Gruyère cheese

1 (17.3-ounce) package prepared puff pastry (2 sheets), thawed overnight in the refrigerator

3 tablespoons grainy Dijon mustard

6 ounces sliced Black Forest ham

1 large egg

1 tablespoon everything bagel seasoning

RIFF
There are countless ways to riff! Turkey and Swiss! Salami and provolone! Sprinkle chocolate chips in the middle to make a giant pain au chocolat!

SERVES 6

My favorite Saturday activity is to drive down to Big Sur first thing in the morning and head straight to Big Sur Bakery, an institution around here. Their ham and cheese croissant is transcendent—the perfectly flaky, buttery croissant layers are wrapped around ham and cheese—it's gorgeous and enormous and one of the best things I've ever tasted. It's well worth waiting in line the next time you find yourself in Northern California, but until then, make my sheet pan version at home for brunch or a fun breakfast for dinner. It looks both elegant and like a massive party when it comes out of the oven.

1. Preheat the oven to 425°F.

2. Grate the **Gruyère**. Unroll each sheet of **puff pastry** on a separate sheet of parchment paper. Using a rolling pin (or a wine bottle!), roll them out as flat as you can, being sure they're as close in size as possible.

3. Spread the **mustard** over one sheet of the pastry, leaving a 1-inch border all around. Add the **ham** in a single layer, then sprinkle on the Gruyère.

4. In a small bowl, whisk together the **egg** and **a tiny splash of water**. Brush the border of the loaded pastry with egg wash. Use the parchment to flip the empty pastry sheet on top of the cheese and lightly press the edges together to seal. Remove the parchment. Cut 3 long slits in the top pastry, then brush the egg wash all over and sprinkle with **everything bagel seasoning**.

5. Bake for 20 to 25 minutes, rotating the pan halfway through, until golden brown and puffed up.

6. Let the pastry cool for several minutes, then cut into even squares and serve.

GRILLED PORK STEAK COCONUT RICE BOWLS

FOR THE GRILLED PORK
¾ cup pineapple-orange juice
   (or orange juice)
¾ cup low-sodium soy sauce
¼ cup neutral oil
3 tablespoons gochujang or
   sriracha
2 garlic cloves
1 (1-inch) piece fresh ginger
1½ to 2 pounds boneless pork
   blade steaks

FOR THE COCONUT RICE
1½ cups sushi rice, rinsed
1 (13.5-ounce) can full-fat
   coconut milk
1 tablespoon sugar
Pinch of kosher salt

TO SERVE
1 (8- to 10-ounce) bag
   shredded green cabbage or
   coleslaw mix
¼ teaspoon kosher salt
Toppings (optional): thinly
   sliced radishes, thinly sliced
   scallions or onion, sesame
   seeds, chopped roasted
   peanuts, shredded carrots

TIPS
If you can't find pork blade steaks, ask the butcher to cut a boneless shoulder into 1-inch steaks.

No grill? Cook the steaks on an indoor grill pan or in a cast-iron skillet. Warm 1 tablespoon oil over medium-high heat, pat the steaks totally dry, and cook for 3 to 4 minutes per side.

SWAP
This marinade is also delicious on chicken, halibut, or shrimp.

SERVES 4 TO 6
Boneless pork blade steaks are thinly sliced slabs of pork butt or shoulder, a cut of pork that is traditionally reserved for longer, slower roasts due to how fatty it is. But when sliced thinly and thrown over a super hot grill for just a few minutes per side, the fatty meat crisps up on the outside, stays so juicy on the inside, and might just become your new favorite cut of meat. Paired with my famous coconut rice, this meal is easy enough to pull off on a weeknight, but impressive enough for a dinner party!

1. **Make the grilled pork:** In a blender, combine the **pineapple-orange juice**, **soy sauce**, **oil**, **gochujang**, **garlic**, and **ginger** (no need to peel it). Blend on high speed until smooth, 30 to 45 seconds.

2. Place the **pork steaks** in a resealable plastic bag or large bowl. Add enough marinade just to cover the pork (about half the marinade). Let marinate at room temperature for at least 30 minutes, or in the refrigerator for up to 24 hours. Cover and refrigerate the remaining marinade (which will become your sauce) until dinnertime.

3. Heat an outdoor grill to high (450° to 500°F).

4. **Meanwhile, make the coconut rice:** In a small pot, combine the **rice**, **coconut milk**, **1 cup water**, the **sugar**, and the **salt**. Bring to a boil over high heat, then reduce the heat to as low as possible, cover, and cook until all the liquid is absorbed, 15 to 17 minutes. Remove the pot from the heat and give it a big stir, then cover and leave the rice to steam for at least 5 minutes or up to 1 hour.

5. Remove the pork from the marinade, allowing excess to drip off (discard the marinade remaining in the bag). Grill over direct heat until charred on the outside and an instant-read thermometer inserted into the thickest part registers 145°F, 3 to 5 minutes per side. Transfer the pork to a cutting board to rest for at least 5 minutes, then slice it against the grain as thinly as possible.

6. Place the **cabbage** in a large bowl and sprinkle it with the **salt**. Using your hands, massage the cabbage to soften it. Stir in 3 to 4 tablespoons of the reserved marinade and toss to coat, adding more as desired.

7. Build the bowls with as much coconut rice, cabbage slaw, and pork as you please. Add any desired toppings, then drizzle some more marinade over the top to finish.

SHEET PAN CHICKEN POBLANO FAJITAS

2 poblano peppers
1 large red onion
2 pounds boneless, skinless chicken thighs
¼ cup neutral oil
1 tablespoon kosher salt, plus more as needed
2 teaspoons chili powder
2 teaspoons ground cumin
1½ teaspoons garlic powder
1 teaspoon smoked paprika
¼ teaspoon cayenne pepper (optional)
8 to 12 (6-inch) flour or corn tortillas
1 lime
10 cilantro sprigs
Toppings (optional): diced avocado, pico de gallo, more cilantro, sour cream, hot sauce

RIFF
Use any leftovers to make taco-dillas (see page 160). Chop them finely and use them in place of the beans in that recipe. You could also use the leftovers to make enchiladas, using the recipe on page 135 as a guide.

SWAP
Use flank steak instead of chicken (only cook it for the last 20 minutes). Try bell peppers and/or zucchini and mushrooms instead of the poblanos.

SERVES 4 TO 6
I love any recipe that can satisfy everyone. If you keep the veggies and chicken separate here, you can please carnivores and vegetarians alike. Leave the spices off a few chicken thighs and make them a plain chicken and cheese taco. Or pile the fajitas into a bowl full of lettuce to make a salad. You and your crew will find endless ways to enjoy these simple, flavorful sheet-pan fajitas.

1. Position one rack in the center of the oven and another in the lower third. Preheat to 450°F. Line two rimmed baking sheets with aluminum foil.

2. Thinly slice the **poblanos** and **onion**. On one prepared baking sheet, combine the **chicken**, poblanos, onion, **oil**, **salt**, **chili powder**, **cumin**, **garlic powder**, **paprika**, and **cayenne** (if using). Toss to coat well, then move half the mixture to the other prepared baking sheet, spreading everything into an even layer.

3. Roast for 30 minutes, switching the baking sheets on the racks halfway through, until the chicken is cooked through and the veggies are golden brown. Stack the **tortillas** and wrap in aluminum foil. Place them on the bottom rack for the final 5 minutes of cooking to warm through.

4. Meanwhile, cut the **lime** in half and finely chop the **cilantro**.

5. Let the chicken and veggies rest for a few minutes, then transfer the chicken to a cutting board and transfer everything else back to one pan. Cut the chicken into small pieces, then return it and any collected juices back to the pan along with the cilantro. Squeeze in the juice of the halved lime and toss to mix well. Taste and add more salt as needed.

6. Serve immediately, with the warmed tortillas for loading up and your preferred **toppings** alongside.

THREE ONE-SKILLET CHICKEN & RICE SITUATIONS

Chicken and rice is a classic pairing in almost any type of cuisine. Here, we're jazzing up these blank canvases in three different ways, all cooked together in one skillet. Not only is cleanup easy, but this method also maximizes flavor all the way through the dish.

CHICKEN & GINGERY RICE WITH COCONUT CURRY SAUCE (PAGE 195)

CHICKEN & PESTO RICE WITH ASPARAGUS (PAGE 196)

CHICKEN
BURRITO BOWLS
(PAGE 194)

2¼ cups low-sodium chicken stock

1½ cups long-grain white rice, rinsed

1 (16-ounce) jar salsa

1 (14.5-ounce) can pinto beans, drained and rinsed

2 pounds bone-in, skin-on chicken breasts

Kosher salt and freshly ground black pepper

2 ounces Cotija or feta cheese

Toppings (optional): chopped avocado, shredded iceberg lettuce, more salsa, fresh cilantro, sour cream, pickled red onions, guacamole, pickled jalapeños

SWAP
Swap in boneless, skinless chicken thighs with no alterations, or use boneless, skinless breasts by baking the rice for 10 minutes on its own first, then adding the chicken.

SERVES 4

I love leaning on salsa to help add tons of flavor to recipes with no work on our part. Let's let somebody else do the hard work of cutting up all of those onions, chiles, peppers, herbs, and tomatoes! Here we use a jar of salsa to flavor rice and pinto beans, then bake chicken right on top.

1. Position a rack in the center of the oven and preheat to 375°F.

2. In a 12-inch ovenproof skillet, combine the **stock**, **rice**, **salsa**, and **beans**. Stir to mix well. Bring to a boil over high heat, then turn off the heat, give it a big stir, and nestle the **chicken** into the rice and liquid, skin side up, so that the skin is resting above the liquid. Season the top of the chicken with **salt** and **several grinds of pepper**.

3. Bake, uncovered, for 30 to 35 minutes, until the rice is tender. (The rice on top might look dry from the heat, so be sure to stick a fork in to check the rice underneath the top layer.) Transfer the chicken to a cutting board and let it rest for 5 minutes. Use a fork to fluff the rice. Cover it to keep warm.

4. When the chicken is cool enough to handle, flip it over to expose the bones. Use your fingers to pull the bones off the breast, then cut the meat into ½-inch-thick slices.

5. Divide the rice and chicken among bowls and serve with the crumbled **Cotija** and any other desired toppings.

ONE-SKILLET CHICKEN & GINGERY RICE
with Coconut Curry Sauce

FOR THE CHICKEN AND RICE
Neutral oil
1½ cups long-grain white rice, rinsed
1 (2-inch) piece fresh ginger
Kosher salt
2 pounds boneless, skinless chicken thighs, fat trimmed

FOR THE COCONUT CURRY SAUCE
Neutral oil
2 tablespoons red curry paste
1 (13.5-ounce) can full-fat coconut milk
2 tablespoons low-sodium soy sauce
1 tablespoon fish sauce
2 teaspoons honey (or sugar)

10 cilantro sprigs, for serving

RIFF Stir 1 tablespoon peanut butter and 1 tablespoon sriracha into the coconut curry sauce to make a spicy peanut curry sauce.

SERVES 4

This dish cooks like a reverse chicken curry. The chicken and rice are seasoned with a simple combo of salt, pepper, and ginger, then cooked in a covered pot, so you can focus on making an insanely flavorful curry sauce that gets drizzled over everything before serving.

1. **Make the chicken and rice:** Warm **1 tablespoon oil** in a 12-inch cast-iron skillet over medium heat. When it shimmers, add the **rice** and grate in the **ginger** (no need to peel it). Cook, stirring, until very fragrant, 2 to 3 minutes. Stir in **2½ cups water** and **¾ teaspoon salt**. Bring to a simmer, then reduce the heat to low.

2. Season the **chicken** thighs with **1½ teaspoons salt**. Lay them over the rice, overlapping slightly if needed to fit. Cover and cook for 20 to 25 minutes, until the rice is tender and an instant-read thermometer inserted into the thickest part of the chicken registers 165°F.

3. Remove the skillet from the heat and let sit, covered, for 10 minutes to allow the rice to steam.

4. **While the chicken and rice are cooking, make the coconut curry sauce:** Warm **1 tablespoon oil** in a small pot over medium heat. When it shimmers, add the **red curry paste** and cook, stirring, until very fragrant and sticking to the bottom of the pot, about 1 minute. Stir in the **coconut milk**, **soy sauce**, **fish sauce**, and **honey**. Increase the heat to high and bring to a boil, then reduce the heat to medium and cook, stirring often, until very thick, like heavy cream or a thin yogurt, 7 to 10 minutes. Remove the pot from the heat and let cool a bit.

5. Chop the **cilantro** and scatter it around the chicken and rice. Drizzle the sauce over the top and serve family-style.

ONE-SKILLET CHICKEN & PESTO RICE
with Asparagus

2 pounds bone-in, skin-on chicken thighs
Kosher salt and freshly ground black pepper
1 large shallot
4 garlic cloves
2¼ cups low-sodium chicken stock
1½ cups long-grain white rice, rinsed
¼ cup pesto, plus more for drizzling
2 lemons
1 pound asparagus
1 tablespoon extra-virgin olive oil
⅓ cup crumbled feta cheese

SWAP
Swap in 2 tablespoons harissa for the pesto for a spiced-up version. Dollop sour cream on top.

SERVES 4

In Carmel Valley, seemingly everyone has a backyard garden, so friends and neighbors are always dropping by with bundles of herbs they've clipped to give away. When you have a surplus of herbs, make a huge batch of pesto and freeze it in an ice cube tray for use all year long. This is one of my favorite ways to make pesto the star of a dish.

1. Position a rack in the center of the oven and preheat to 375°F.

2. Pat the **chicken** dry, then season it all over with **1½ teaspoons salt** and **¼ teaspoon pepper**.

3. Thinly slice the **shallot** and **garlic**. Warm a 12-inch ovenproof skillet over medium heat. When you flick a drop of water into it and it dances around the pan, it's hot enough. Arrange the chicken thighs in the skillet skin side down. Sear for 3 to 4 minutes, until the fat begins to render, then add the shallot and garlic around the chicken. Season the shallot with a **pinch of salt**. Cook the chicken, undisturbed but moving the shallots and garlic around, until the chicken skin is golden and releases easily from the pan, about 15 minutes.

4. Flip the chicken skin side up. Pour in the **stock**, and add the **rice**, **pesto**, and **¼ teaspoon salt**. Halve **1 lemon** and squeeze the juice into the skillet. Use tongs to evenly spread the rice and liquid around the chicken. Increase the heat to high and bring to a boil, then transfer the skillet to the oven.

5. Roast for 15 minutes, or until the rice has absorbed much of the liquid.

6. Meanwhile, cut the **asparagus** into 1-inch pieces. Cut the remaining **lemon** into 6 wedges.

7. Scatter the chopped asparagus over the top of the skillet, drizzle it with the **olive oil**, and season it with a **big pinch of salt**. Roast for 10 minutes more, until the asparagus is crisp-tender, the rice is tender, and an instant-read thermometer inserted into the thickest part of the chicken registers 165°F.

8. Garnish with the **feta** and a drizzle of pesto. Serve with the lemon wedges alongside for squeezing.

CRISPY ROSEMARY CHICKEN
with Schmaltzy Balsamic Cabbage

1 head purple cabbage (about
    2 pounds)
Extra-virgin olive oil
¼ cup balsamic vinegar, plus
    more for drizzling
Kosher salt and freshly ground
    black pepper
2 rosemary sprigs
4 chicken leg quarters (about
    4 pounds total)
1 teaspoon garlic powder

RIFF
Kielbasa and Cabbage: Roast the cabbage for 40 minutes, then add kielbasa (cut into 3-inch pieces) on top and roast for 15 minutes more. Serve with some grainy mustard.

SWAP
You can use any cut of chicken here—boneless will be done in 20 to 25 minutes. Remember, the meat thermometer is your best friend! Just pull the chicken off the baking sheet and continue cooking the cabbage.

SERVES 4

We are a family of roast chicken lovers, and no recipe makes the rotation in our home as much as this one. The chicken is crispy and juicy, but the real star here is the cabbage. George and I can easily eat an entire head of cabbage when it's cooked this way—roasted to perfection in chicken schmaltz (aka chicken fat) and balsamic, it's sweet, savory, tangy—you won't believe the speed with which you manage to inhale cabbage.

1. Preheat the oven to 450°F.

2. Thinly slice the **cabbage**. On a rimmed baking sheet, toss the cabbage with **¼ cup olive oil**, the **vinegar**, **1½ teaspoons salt**, and **several grinds of pepper**.

3. Roast for 15 minutes, until the cabbage has begun to soften a bit.

4. Meanwhile, strip the leaves off the **rosemary sprigs**, then mince the leaves as finely as you possibly can. Season the **chicken** all over with **2 tablespoons olive oil**, **1½ teaspoons salt**, the **garlic powder**, and **several grinds of pepper**. Press about 1 tablespoon of the minced rosemary into the chicken skin.

5. Add the chicken directly on top of the cabbage and roast for 40 to 45 minutes, until an instant-read thermometer inserted into the chicken registers 165°F.

6. Divide the chicken among four plates, then stir the cabbage on the baking sheet to toss it in all the chicken fat (it will be very wet!). Increase the oven temperature to 500°F and return the baking sheet to the oven for 10 minutes while the chicken rests.

7. Add the cabbage to the plates with the chicken. Drizzle with a little more balsamic vinegar and serve.

KINDA MARBELLA

2 (1- to 1½-pound) pork tenderloins
Kosher salt and freshly ground black pepper
2 tablespoons extra-virgin olive oil
1 fennel bulb
4 garlic cloves
1½ cups dates
¼ cup fresh parsley leaves and tender stems
1½ cups dry white wine (I like sauvignon blanc)
½ cup red wine vinegar or balsamic vinegar
⅓ cup maple syrup
1½ cups pitted green olives
3 tablespoons unsalted butter
1 cup couscous (see Learn)

LEARN
While it has its time and place, you do *not* want to use Israeli couscous here! If you buy that accidentally, just cook it per the package instructions and serve it alongside. It'll be great too, but it has a totally different cooking method.

SWAP
Make chicken Marbella using boneless, skinless chicken breasts instead. They'll require slightly less cook time—use an instant-read thermometer and pull them out when they hit 165°F.

SERVES 4 TO 6

The Silver Palate Cookbook is a classic that was always on my kitchen counter growing up, dog-eared and covered in smudges from my mom's constant use of it. In my opinion, the most famous, best dish from the 1980s cookbook is the chicken Marbella. It's fabulous, but it requires an overnight marinade and a much longer cook time. Using pork tenderloin allows you to do things much more quickly for a fancy-feeling one-skillet weeknight meal. I make a few other swaps, too—adding fennel for some veg, dates instead of prunes because I *love* dates—so this my a kinda-Marbella adaptation.

1. Preheat the oven to 400°F.

2. Pat the **pork tenderloins** dry and season all over with **1 teaspoon salt** and **several grinds of pepper**.

3. Warm the **olive oil** in a 12-inch ovenproof skillet over medium-high heat. When it shimmers, add the tenderloins (cut them in half or just curve them around to fit them in the skillet) and sear until a golden brown crust forms on the bottom, 3 to 4 minutes.

4. Meanwhile, thinly slice the **fennel** and mince the **garlic**.

5. Flip the pork, add the fennel and garlic to the pan, and cook, leaving the pork undisturbed but stirring around the fennel and garlic, until the second side is seared, another 3 to 4 minutes, then remove the skillet from the heat.

6. Meanwhile, halve the **dates** lengthwise and remove the pits. Finely chop the **parsley**.

7. Add the dates to the skillet along with the **wine**, **vinegar**, **maple syrup**, and **olives**.

8. Transfer the skillet to the oven and roast for 12 to 15 minutes, until an instant-read thermometer inserted into the pork registers 140°F. Transfer the pork to a cutting board and let rest while you make the sauce.

9. Return the skillet to medium-high heat. Stir in **1 tablespoon of the butter** and cook, stirring occasionally, until the sauce thickens slightly, 4 to 5 minutes.

10. While the sauce reduces, combine the remaining **2 tablespoons butter**, **1⅓ cups water**, and a **big pinch of salt** in a small saucepan. Bring to a boil over high heat, then remove from the heat, stir in the **couscous**, and cover. Let sit until the couscous has absorbed all the water, about 5 minutes.

11. Cut the pork into ¼-inch-thick slices. Arrange on a platter and spoon the sauce over the top. Top with the parsley and serve with the couscous alongside.

COUSCOUS:
the fastest, easiest side dish

THOUGH IT LOOKS AND ACTS A LOT LIKE A GRAIN, COUSCOUS IS, IN FACT, TINY BALLS OF SEMOLINA FLOUR AND WATER, AKA TINY BITS OF PASTA. IT MAKES A FANTASTIC QUICK-AND-EASY SIDE DISH, ESPECIALLY FOR A SAUCY DISH. JUST COMBINE IT WITH HOT WATER OR STOCK, COVER, LET IT STEAM FOR 5 MINUTES, AND YOU'VE GOT PERFECTLY FLUFFY COUSCOUS.

PLAIN JANE COUSCOUS
1 cup couscous + 1 1/4 cups hot water + 1 tablespoon olive oil + 1/2 teaspoon kosher salt

GOLDEN COUSCOUS PILAF
1 cup couscous + 1 1/4 cups hot water + 1/3 cup golden raisins + 2 tablespoons chopped fresh parsley + 3/4 teaspoon ground turmeric + 1/2 teaspoon kosher salt

LEMON PEPPER COUSCOUS
1 cup couscous + 1 cup hot water or stock + the zest and juice of 1 lemon + 1 tablespoon butter + 1/2 teaspoon kosher salt + 1/4 teaspoon freshly ground black pepper

HERBY COUSCOUS
1 cup couscous + 1 1/4 cups cup hot stock + 1 tablespoon butter + 1/2 teaspoon kosher salt + 1/2 cup finely chopped fresh dill + 1/2 cup finely chopped fresh basil + 1/2 cup chopped pistachios

SKILLET CHEDDAR TURKEY BURGERS

FOR THE BURGERS
1 pound ground turkey
½ cup shredded white cheddar
  cheese
¼ cup mayonnaise
1 teaspoon garlic powder
1 teaspoon chili powder
¾ teaspoon kosher salt
4 scallions

FOR THE BURGER SAUCE/
SALAD DRESSING
½ cup mayonnaise
2 tablespoons hot sauce
Kosher salt
1 lime

1 head iceberg lettuce
1 tablespoon neutral oil
4 burger buns
Potato chips, for serving
  (optional)
Toppings (optional): thinly
  sliced tomato, thinly sliced
  red onion

LEARN
You can grill your burgers if you prefer. Cook them on medium-high heat for 3 to 4 minutes per side. Throw some veggies on there while you're at it!

SERVES 4

I know. Mayo in burger patties. It seems wrong. But trust the process. Turkey is incredibly lean—that's why it dries out so easily. So we are adding mayo (it's just oil and eggs!!! Don't be weird about it!) to the mixture to add a bit of fat to the equation to make them juicy and fabulous. I am always trying to make my ingredient lists as short as possible, so a few years ago, knowing that I wanted a mayo-based sauce to go with my turkey burgers, I tried using mayo instead of eggs to bind the patties, and I've never looked back.

1. **Prep the burgers:** Preheat the oven to 375°F.

2. In a large bowl, combine the **turkey**, **cheese**, **mayonnaise**, **garlic powder**, **chili powder**, and **salt**.

3. Thinly slice the **scallions** and add them to the turkey mixture. Use your hands to mix well, then divide the meat into four thin patties, about ½ inch thick.

4. **Make the burger sauce/salad dressing:** In a small bowl, stir together the **mayo**, **hot sauce**, and a **pinch of salt**. Cut the **lime** in half and squeeze in the juice; stir to combine. Taste and adjust the seasoning as needed.

5. Thinly slice the **iceberg** and place it in a large serving bowl.

6. **Cook the burgers:** Warm your largest nonstick skillet over medium-high heat. When you flick a drop of water into it and it dances around the pan, it's hot enough. Add the **oil** to the pan and swirl to coat the pan evenly. Cook as many patties at a time as you can without having them touch, for 4 to 5 minutes per side, until golden brown all over.

7. When you flip the burgers, throw the **buns** on a baking sheet and place them in the oven to warm them up for the final 4 to 5 minutes.

8. Spread the burger sauce on both sides of the bun, then add a patty to each, along with your desired toppings, including **chips**, if you're into that. Throw ¼ cup of the burger sauce and a **big pinch of salt** into the iceberg and toss to dress it. Serve the burgers with the iceberg (and more chips, if you like) alongside.

SUSHI PARTY

FOR THE SALMON
2 pounds salmon
2 tablespoons low-sodium soy sauce
2 tablespoons sriracha
1 tablespoon maple syrup

FOR THE RICE
2 cups sushi rice, rinsed
1 tablespoon rice vinegar
2 teaspoons maple syrup
½ teaspoon kosher salt

TO SERVE
1 English (hothouse) cucumber
2 large avocados
2 cups packed mixed greens
Pickled ginger
1 (3.5-ounce) package wonton strips
5 nori sheets
½ cup low-sodium soy sauce
1 tablespoon rice vinegar
1 tablespoon plus 1 teaspoon maple syrup
½ cup mayonnaise
2 tablespoons sriracha
6 ounces crabmeat (imitation or real)

TIP The salmon can be marinated ahead, all the sauces can be made ahead, and the crab can be made up to 24 hours in advance.

SHORTCUT Buy tuna poke from a good seafood place and use that instead of the salmon or crab. Use frozen sticky rice to cut out the rice-cooking step. Buy sriracha mayo.

SERVES 4 TO 6

You might be thinking that making a million little components doesn't really adhere to the "what to cook when you DON'T FEEL LIKE COOKING" ethos. But here's the thing: This is an easy recipe, and every component is super simple. Like it or not, there will be nights when you don't feel like cooking, but you're also having people over for dinner and you want to impress them. This is the recipe for that night. It's fun, it's delicious, it's something new. For an easy weeknight meal, choose either the salmon *or* the crab, and use microwaveable frozen rice! To make it even more of a feast, add shrimp, tofu, and/or tuna!

1. **Make the salmon:** Preheat the oven to 225°F. Line a rimmed baking sheet with foil.

2. Place the **salmon** on the prepared baking sheet and rub with the **soy sauce**, **sriracha**, and **maple syrup**. Let marinate at room temperature for at least 10 minutes, or covered in the refrigerator for up to 24 hours.

3. **Meanwhile, make the rice:** Combine the **rice**, **vinegar**, **maple syrup**, **salt**, and **2 cups water** in a medium pot and bring to a boil over high heat. Give it a big stir, then reduce the heat to low, cover, and cook until the rice is tender, 17 to 20 minutes. Turn off the heat and keep covered until you're ready to serve.

4. Bake the salmon for 40 to 50 minutes, until the flesh is opaque and flakes easily or an instant-read thermometer inserted into the thickest part registers 130°F for medium-rare or 140°F for medium.

5. While the salmon bakes, cut the **cucumber** into skinny batons. Thinly slice the **avocados**. Place both on a large serving board or platter, along with a bowl filled with the **mixed greens**, a bowl filled with **pickled ginger**, and a bowl filled with crumbled **wonton strips**. Using kitchen scissors, cut the **nori sheets** into 4 squares each and throw them on the board too.

6. In a small bowl, stir together the **soy sauce**, **vinegar**, and **maple syrup**. In a separate small bowl, stir together the **mayonnaise** and **sriracha**, then place the bowls on the serving board.

7. Break the **crabmeat** into small pieces in a medium bowl and stir in a small spoonful of the sriracha mayo just to moisten it.

8. Place everything on the table and let everyone create their own hand rolls or sushi bowls.

MAPLE-ROASTED SWEET POTATOES & LABNEH

6 (8-ounce) sweet potatoes
3 tablespoons extra-virgin
    olive oil
2 teaspoons maple syrup
1¼ teaspoons kosher salt
1 teaspoon smoked paprika
¾ teaspoon ground cumin
½ teaspoon garlic powder
½ teaspoon ground coriander
1 cup fresh soft herbs, such as
    dill and/or parsley
⅓ cup smoked almonds
Labneh, plain full-fat Greek
    yogurt, or sour cream, for
    serving

RIFF Make stuffed sweet potatoes instead. Roast whole sweet potatoes for 1 hour at the same temperature, then cut them in half and use a fork to fluff them a bit. Top them with labneh, herbs, and almonds.

SWAP Any dense root vegetable is great here. Carrots are delicious cooked this way, as are beets, parsnips, and turnips.

BULK IT UP You could also throw 6 to 8 bone-in, skin-on chicken thighs in there to roast for the final 40 minutes to make it a meat-and-veg dinner.

SERVES 4

Sometimes I just want a big bowl of roasted vegetables, and this meal scratches the itch every single time. Perfectly sweet and savory spiced potatoes are served over creamy labneh, with lots of fresh herbs and crunchy smoked nuts. Every bite has a ton of contrasting fresh and roasty and creamy textures.

1. Preheat the oven to 400°F.

2. Slice the **sweet potatoes** into 1-inch-thick rounds.

3. On a rimmed baking sheet, toss the sweet potatoes with the **olive oil**, **maple syrup**, **salt**, **paprika**, **cumin**, **garlic powder**, and **coriander** to coat evenly.

4. Roast the potatoes for 1 hour, until tender and caramelized.

5. Meanwhile, roughly chop the **herbs** and **almonds**.

6. Smear **labneh** on the bottom of four bowls or plates. Pile the sweet potatoes on top and garnish with the herbs and nuts.

SALMON CRUNCH BOWLS

FOR THE RICE AND SALMON
Kosher salt
1½ cups brown rice
4 tablespoons (½ stick) unsalted butter
4 (6-ounce) skinless salmon fillets
½ teaspoon garlic powder
½ teaspoon ground ginger
1 tablespoon low-sodium soy sauce
1 to 2 tablespoons sriracha
2 tablespoons sesame oil
1 tablespoon maple syrup or brown sugar
¼ cup panko breadcrumbs
3 tablespoons sesame seeds

FOR THE SRIRACHA MAYO
½ cup mayonnaise
1 tablespoon sriracha, plus more as needed
1 lime
Kosher salt

Toppings (optional): mixed greens, chopped cilantro, peanuts, chopped cucumbers, shredded carrots, shredded cabbage

SERVES 4

These salmon crunch bowls are the darling of *What to Cook*, the newsletter, with almost triple the number of comments and likes of any other recipe. Whenever new readers ask which recipe should be the first one they cook, "the salmon" is at the very top of the list. The effort-to-reward ratio on this one is a huge part of its appeal. For a simple weeknight meal, I just serve it with rice and some cucumbers, but for a dinner party, I go all out, offering every crunchy veggie under the sun, to allow people to build their own perfect bowl.

1. **Make the rice and salmon:** Bring a large pot of salted water to a boil over high heat. Add the **rice** and cook, uncovered, until tender, about 40 minutes. Drain, then return the rice to the pot and stir in **2 tablespoons of the butter** and a **big pinch of salt**. Cover until you're ready to eat.

2. Preheat the oven to 400°F. Line a rimmed baking sheet with parchment paper.

3. Place the **salmon** on the prepared sheet. Sprinkle it with **1 teaspoon salt**, the **garlic powder**, and **ginger**, then rub with the **soy sauce**, **sriracha**, **1 tablespoon of the sesame oil**, and the **maple syrup**.

4. In a medium bowl, melt the remaining **2 tablespoons butter** in the microwave for 20 seconds. Add the remaining **1 tablespoon sesame oil**, the **panko**, **sesame seeds**, and a **big pinch of salt**. Stir the panko mixture until combined.

5. Spread the panko over the top of the salmon. Bake for 15 to 18 minutes, until the salmon easily flakes when you prod at it with a fork.

6. **Meanwhile, make the sriracha mayo:** In a small bowl, stir together the **mayo** and **sriracha**. Halve the **lime** and juice one half into the mayo mixture; cut the remaining half into wedges for serving. Season the sriracha mayo with a **small pinch of salt**. Taste and add more sriracha if you want it spicier.

7. Now set everything out and let everyone build their own bowls!

TIP
The salmon can be fully assembled and thrown in the fridge until you're 20 minutes from when you want to serve dinner, then baked.

RIFF
This is one of my favorite dinner party meals—I buy a 2- to 3-pound salmon side (aka one huge slab of salmon), triple the seasonings and crunchy topping, and roast it whole.

SWAP
Halibut, trout, or even cod are great in place of the salmon. Just adjust the cooking time accordingly (a bit more for halibut, similar for trout, a bit less for cod).

CREAMY CREAMLESS TOMATO SOUP
with Cheesy Salty Honey Toast

FOR THE SOUP
4 garlic cloves
4 tablespoons (½ stick) unsalted butter, or ¼ cup extra-virgin olive oil
¼ cup tomato paste
1 medium sweet potato
2 (28-ounce) cans whole peeled tomatoes
2 cups low-sodium vegetable stock, plus more as needed
½ cup cashews (preferably raw)
2 teaspoons kosher salt, plus more as needed
¼ teaspoon freshly ground black pepper, plus more as needed
2 tablespoons honey, plus more as needed

FOR THE TOAST
8 slices sourdough bread
8 ounces any shredded cheese you like
Honey, for drizzling
Flaky sea salt, for serving

LEARN
You *can* use an immersion blender here—but you won't get the creamy, smooth consistency we're going for, so I don't recommend it.

SWAP
For a cashew allergy, swap in 1/2 cup canned cannellini beans.

SLOW
To make the soup in a slow cooker, add all the ingredients, cover, and cook on low for 6 hours. Use an immersion blender to blend right in the cooker (despite my note directly above), then keep it warm in there until you're ready to eat.

SERVES 6

Tomato soup with grilled cheese is the dictionary definition of America's comfort food—but it can be a bit heavy, with the cream in the soup and the cheesy sandwiches. Enter this tomato soup recipe, which relies on two surprise ingredients: sweet potatoes for sweetness and cashews for creaminess. Then pair it with an open-faced cheesy salty honey toast that is best when dunked. Everyone will like it even better than the OG!

1. **Make the soup:** Finely grate the **garlic** directly into a large pot. Add the **butter** and **tomato paste** and cook, stirring, over medium heat until the tomato paste has darkened, 5 to 7 minutes.

2. Meanwhile, peel and chop the **sweet potato** into big chunks.

3. Add the sweet potato to the pot, along with the **tomatoes**, **stock**, **cashews**, **salt**, and **pepper**. Increase the heat to high and bring to a boil, then reduce the heat to medium-low, cover, and cook for 45 minutes, until the sweet potatoes and cashews are very tender.

4. Stir in the **honey** and let the soup cool for a few minutes. Working in batches, transfer to a high-powered blender (don't fill the blender more than three-quarters of the way) and blend on high speed for 1 minute, until totally smooth. Return the blended soup to the pot. If it's too thick, simply blend in a bit more stock (up to 2 more cups) until it reaches a nice bisque-ish consistency.

5. Taste and add more salt, pepper, and honey (if it tastes too acidic) as needed. Simmer the soup over low heat while you make the toast.

6. **Make the toast:** Position a rack at the top of the oven and heat the broiler to high.

7. Arrange the **bread** on a baking sheet. Sprinkle the **cheese** over the tops, dividing it evenly. Drizzle with a little bit of **honey**. Just before serving, broil until the cheese is melted, 3 to 4 minutes. Shower with a **big pinch of flaky salt**.

8. Ladle the soup into bowls and serve with the cheesy honey toast alongside.

MELTY MEXICAN CAULIFLOWER

1 large head cauliflower (see
Shortcut, page 88)
1 tablespoon chili powder
1 teaspoon smoked paprika
1 teaspoon ground cumin
3 tablespoons extra-virgin
olive oil
Kosher salt
1 (15-ounce) can black beans
¼ teaspoon garlic powder
½ bunch cilantro
½ cup sour cream
3 tablespoons Mexican hot
sauce (I like Cholula)
1 cup shredded Monterey Jack
cheese
¼ cup pickled jalapeños
½ cup pico de gallo
Handful of tortilla chips

SHORTCUT
Instead
of measuring out all the
individual spices listed,
just use 1 tablespoon plus
2 teaspoons of taco seasoning
and reduce the salt to
1/2 teaspoon.

SWAP
I mean, let's call
it what it is: Instead of
cauliflower, layer tortilla
chips with all these
ingredients for traditional
nachos.

SERVES 2 TO 4

A lesser person might call this dish "cauliflower nachos," but I refuse. Cauliflower has had a hard enough time lately—being turned into pizza crusts and bread and crackers—it doesn't need the added pressure of being expected to replace tortilla chips. No, this recipe is just a delightful way to enjoy cauliflower that happens to have been heavily influenced by nachos. George and I can easily polish off a sheet pan of these by ourselves, so I highly recommend serving these over a nice bowl of buttery rice if you're feeding four.

1. Preheat the oven to 450°F. Line a rimmed baking sheet with parchment paper.

2. Core the **cauliflower** and cut it into florets. Combine the **chili powder**, **paprika**, and **cumin** in a small bowl.

3. On the prepared baking sheet, toss the cauliflower with the **olive oil**, 1 tablespoon of the spice mix (see Shortcut), and **1 teaspoon salt**. Bake for 35 to 40 minutes, until very tender and golden brown.

4. Meanwhile, dump the **black beans and their liquid** into a small pot. Add **2 tablespoons water**, the remaining 2 teaspoons spice mix, the **garlic powder**, **4 cilantro sprigs**, and a **pinch of salt**. Bring to a boil over high heat, then reduce the heat to medium-low and cook, stirring occasionally, until the beans are nice and thick and not at all liquidy, about 10 minutes. Pick out and discard the cilantro sprigs, then smash the beans against the side of the pot a bit.

5. In a small bowl, stir together the **sour cream**, **hot sauce**, and a **pinch of salt**. Taste and adjust the seasoning as needed.

6. Scooch the cauliflower florets together in the center of the baking sheet so they're all touching, then scatter the beans and **cheese** (use more, if ya want!) over the top. Bake until the cheese has melted, about 10 minutes more.

7. Meanwhile, finely chop the remaining **cilantro**.

8. Drizzle some spicy crema all over everything, then sprinkle around the **jalapeños**, **pico de gallo**, chopped cilantro, and the **tortilla chips**, crumbling them in your hands as you go. Serve with the rest of the crema alongside for dipping.

PIMENTO CHEESE EVERYTHING BAGEL GALETTE

1 pound of the ripest, most delicious tomatoes you can find

Kosher salt and freshly ground black pepper

1 refrigerated prepared piecrust (not the kind in the tin, the kind that comes in a roll)

⅓ cup plus 1 tablespoon mayonnaise

¼ teaspoon garlic powder

1 lemon

1 (4-ounce) jar diced pimentos, drained

1¼ cups shredded sharp cheddar cheese

2 to 3 teaspoons everything bagel seasoning

¼ cup fresh basil leaves

RIFF
Make a zucchini galette by grating 3 large zucchini, then placing them in a colander. Toss with a big pinch of salt and let drain for 15 minutes. Then throw it in a kitchen towel and use your hands to continue squeezing out excess moisture. Pile the grated zucchini over the cheese in place of the tomatoes, then bake as directed.

SHORTCUT
Use store-bought pimento cheese, spread it on the piecrust, and top with tomatoes.

SERVES 4

I've been making this galette for years and years, and people lose their minds over it every time. The combination of perfectly acidic and sweet summer tomatoes, creamy mayo and cheese, buttery crust, and savory everything bagel seasoning is an addictive combo. It's great to bring to a potluck, or the perfect solution when you're asked to bring an appetizer to a party.

1. Preheat the oven to 400°F. Line a baking sheet with parchment paper.

2. Cut the **tomatoes** into ¼-inch-thick slices and lay them out on a double layer of paper towels. Sprinkle them liberally with **salt** and let sit for 20 minutes to release their liquid.

3. Lay out the **piecrust** on the prepared baking sheet. Spread **⅓ cup of the mayonnaise** over the piecrust, leaving a 1½-inch border. Sprinkle the mayonnaise with **¼ teaspoon salt**, the **garlic powder**, and several grinds of **pepper**. Grate the zest of the **lemon** over as well. Scatter the **pimentos** all over, then **1 cup of the cheddar**.

4. Pat the tops of the tomatoes with paper towels until you've removed as much moisture as possible. Beginning in the center of the crust, layer the tomatoes in a circular pattern over the cheese, leaving a 1-inch border.

5. Fold the crust border over the tomatoes. If the piecrust rips or doesn't fit perfectly, no worries! Just pinch it back together and scooch the tomatoes around to make it work. Sprinkle the remaining **¼ cup cheddar** over the tomatoes. Using your fingers, spread the remaining **1 tablespoon mayonnaise** over the exposed piecrust, then sprinkle the **everything bagel seasoning** over the mayo.

6. Bake for 40 to 50 minutes, until the crust is light brown. Let rest for at least 5 minutes.

7. Meanwhile, thinly slice the **basil**.

8. Sprinkle the galette with a little salt and pepper and top with the basil. Cut into triangles and enjoy hot or at room temperature.

LOW-EFFORT MUSHROOM RISOTTO

1 medium yellow onion
3 tablespoons extra-virgin
   olive oil, plus more as needed
1 pound mushrooms (any kind),
   thinly sliced
Kosher salt and freshly ground
   black pepper
1½ cups Arborio rice
4 cups low-sodium chicken
   stock, plus more as needed
3 ounces Gruyère cheese, plus
   more for serving
½ cup dry white wine (such as
   sauvignon blanc)
1½ cups frozen peas
2 tablespoons unsalted butter
Juice of ½ lemon

SLOW
To make this in a slow cooker, throw the onion, mushrooms, rice, stock, salt, pepper, and wine in the crock, cover, and cook on low for 4 hours. Uncover and stir in the peas, butter, lemon juice, and Gruyère, then cook, uncovered, for 30 minutes more.

BULK IT UP
Spinach is delicious in this risotto—stir in a few handfuls when you add the peas.

SWAP
If you aren't into Gruyère, Parm or white cheddar is great here instead.

SERVES 4

I've been making Queen Ina's oven-baked risotto for as long as I can remember. (That's Ina Garten, in case you're new to . . . the world?) When I owned a catering company, her recipe was ideal because I could pop it in the oven, work on all the other dishes, and simply pull it out when it was time to serve. I'd have a gorgeous risotto to show off, without fail. I've riffed on hers in many ways over the years, but this mushroom version is my family's favorite.

1. Position a rack in the center of the oven and preheat to 350°F.

2. Dice the **onion**. Warm the **olive oil** in a large Dutch oven over medium-high heat. When it shimmers, add the **mushrooms** and stir to coat in the oil. Spread them into an even layer and cook, undisturbed, for 3 minutes, then stir, spread evenly again, and cook, undisturbed, for 3 minutes more. Add more oil if the skillet gets too dry. Stir in the onions and cook until slightly softened, about 3 minutes. If the mushrooms or onions are burning, turn down the heat, but cooking them over high heat will help their moisture evaporate and let them brown quickly! Add **1 teaspoon salt** and **¼ teaspoon pepper** and stir until the mushrooms and onions are very tender and browned.

3. Add the **rice** and cook, stirring, until lightly toasted, about 1 minute. Pour in the **stock**, increase the heat to high, and bring to a boil. Give it a big stir to dislodge any bits stuck to the bottom.

4. Cover the pot, transfer to the oven, and bake until the liquid is absorbed and the rice is tender, about 45 minutes. Meanwhile, grate the **Gruyère**.

5. Remove from the oven, return the pot to the stovetop over medium-low heat, and stir in the **wine** until completely absorbed, 2 to 3 minutes. Stir in the **peas**, **butter**, **lemon juice**, and Gruyère. Cook, stirring continuously, until the cheese is melted and everything is looking delish, 2 to 3 minutes. You might want to add more stock or water (up to 1 cup) depending on how your rice is absorbing the liquid. The risotto should be saucy and loose, not thick and gloopy.

6. Divide the risotto among four bowls and top each with an extra sprinkle of Gruyère.

A LITTLE
BIT LONGER

SLOW-COOKED BBQ RIBS & RANCH-Y POTATOES

2 (3- to 4-pound) racks baby back ribs
2 tablespoons brown sugar
Kosher salt and freshly ground black pepper
1 teaspoon chili powder
3 pounds Dutch yellow potatoes
¼ cup extra-virgin olive oil
2 tablespoon apple cider vinegar
1½ teaspoons dried dill
1 teaspoon garlic powder
1 cup barbecue sauce (I like Stubb's), plus more for dipping
Flaky sea salt

RIFF
Try brushing one of the racks of ribs with a store-bought teriyaki sauce or miso-maple glaze (see page 229) to give your diners two options.

BULK IT UP
For a traditional Southern BBQ feast, make some mac and cheese and slaw to serve with everything.

SERVES 4 TO 6

Cooking ribs seems like a "project," but with this recipe, they're a simple set-it-and-forget-it dinner. This is a really fun celebratory meal—it's George's request every Father's Day. I let the kids help me set the table outside, with flowers picked from the yard, and then I grab some local IPAs and throw on a bluegrass playlist to make it feel extra special.

1. Place one rack in the center of the oven and another in the bottom third. Preheat to 275°F. Line one rimmed baking sheet with aluminum foil and a second with parchment paper.

2. Place the **ribs** on the foil-lined baking sheet. Pat them completely dry. Season all over with the **brown sugar**, **1 tablespoon kosher salt**, **1½ teaspoons pepper**, and the **chili powder**. Cover tightly with foil. Roast on the center rack for 2 hours.

3. Meanwhile, quarter the **potatoes**. On the parchment-lined baking sheet, toss them with the **olive oil**, **vinegar**, **2 teaspoons salt**, the **dill**, **garlic powder**, and **several grinds of pepper**.

4. After the ribs have been cooking for 2 hours, add the potatoes to the oven on the bottom rack. Continue roasting together for 45 minutes.

5. Increase the oven temperature to 450°F. Remove the foil from the ribs and pour off any excess moisture from the baking sheet. Generously brush the tops of the ribs with a coating of **barbecue sauce**. Return the ribs to the oven and cook for 25 to 30 minutes more, until the sauce has caramelized and the potatoes are crispy on the outside and creamy on the inside. Remove both baking sheets from the oven. Let the ribs rest for at least 5 minutes. Sprinkle the potatoes with **flaky salt**.

6. Cut the racks into individual ribs by slicing between the bones. Serve with more barbecue sauce alongside for dipping.

SHORT RIBS
with Fresh Corn Polenta

2 cups jarred marinara sauce (I like Rao's)

¾ cup red wine (I like Justin pinot noir)

¼ cup red wine vinegar

3 pounds beef short ribs

Kosher salt

16 ounces frozen white corn, thawed

⅓ cup milk or cream (or just use water!)

2 tablespoons unsalted butter

¾ teaspoon sugar

Freshly ground black pepper

Finely chopped fresh soft herbs, such as parsley or basil, for serving (optional)

SWAP
If you can't find short ribs, grab a big piece of beef chuck and cut it into 3-inch cubes. Bake for an initial 2 1/2 hours instead of 3, and continue with the recipe as written.

SERVES 4

My least favorite part of braising big hunks of meat is taking the time to properly sear it before adding liquid to the pot. It takes forever! Grease splatters all over my kitchen! So here we skip the sear, opting for a method in which the meat is slightly exposed during the braise, thus gaining those same crispy bits we all crave. Chopping a million vegetables to make the braising liquid for my short ribs is also a downer. To get the same amount of flavor without the effort, you'll use good marinara sauce, which has already done all of that hard work for you. Two perfect shortcuts, one perfect meal.

1. Preheat the oven to 250°F.

2. In a 12-inch ovenproof skillet or 9 x 13-inch baking dish, combine the **marinara sauce**, **red wine**, and **vinegar**. Season the **short ribs** with **2½ teaspoons salt**, then nestle them into the sauce, bone side up.

3. Bake for 3 hours, then turn the ribs onto their side and cook for another hour. If the sauce becomes too dark or looks like it might burn, stir in ⅓ cup water. Turn the ribs onto their other side and cook for an additional 1 to 1½ hours, until the meat is fork-tender.

4. When about 15 minutes remain, combine the **corn** and the **milk** in a blender. Blend on high speed until smooth, 45 seconds to 1 minute.

5. Pour the blended corn into a medium skillet along with the **butter**, **sugar**, **¾ teaspoon salt**, and **several grinds of pepper**. Cook over medium-low heat, stirring occasionally, until thickened to the consistency of polenta, 5 to 10 minutes.

6. Carefully spoon off and discard the oily fat layer from the top of the short ribs.

7. Divide the corn among bowls. Use tongs to place the short ribs on top (the bones might fall off; just discard them if they do). Spoon lots of sauce over the top. Garnish with some green **herbs** if you feel like it, but, meh, you've waited long enough!

TURKEY BOLOGNESE
with Sneaky Veggies

2 medium carrots
2 celery stalks
1 small yellow onion
4 garlic cloves
2 tablespoons unsalted butter
2 cups cauliflower rice (fresh or frozen)
2 teaspoons dried oregano
¼ teaspoon red pepper flakes
⅛ teaspoon ground nutmeg
1 pound ground turkey
1 (14.5-ounce) can diced tomatoes
1 (14.5-ounce) can tomato puree
1 tablespoon kosher salt, plus more as needed
½ cup half-and-half
1 lemon
1 pound pasta (I like a tubular pasta like rigatoni)
½ cup freshly grated Parmesan cheese, plus more as needed
Freshly ground black pepper

SHORTCUT
When I don't have time to make this recipe from scratch, I just cook the cauliflower rice, chopped veggies, and ground turkey as above, then stir in a 28-ounce jar of Rao's marinara sauce and stir it over medium-high heat until it's thick and delicious, 5 to 10 minutes.

SLOW
To make this in a slow cooker, cook the veggies and turkey in a skillet as directed, then transfer to the slow cooker and add the remaining ingredients. Cover and cook on high for 4 hours, then uncover and cook until the sauce thickens up, about 30 minutes more.

SERVES 8 TO 10

When people talk about "kid-friendly" meals, I always scoff. There's no such thing as a kid-friendly meal! One day my five-year-old will tell me that his favorite food in the entire world forever and ever is chicken fingers. The next, he won't touch them because they're "so yucky and dee-skus-ting." All that is to say: This is the meal that I make when I need to feed a large crowd of adults and kids, and I want it to be a smashing success, no last-minute PB&Js required. It's packed with hidden veggies, and it (almost) never fails me as a cross-generational crowd-pleaser. When I make this recipe, I always double it! Freeze half of the sauce in a zip-top bag for a day when you really don't feel like cooking.

1. Roughly chop the **carrots**, **celery**, and **onion** and place them in a food processor or blender. Add the **garlic** and pulse until very finely chopped, about 15 pulses. (Alternatively, you can finely chop them by hand.)

2. Melt the **butter** in a large Dutch oven or wide pot over medium-high heat. Add the chopped vegetables, **cauliflower rice**, **oregano**, **red pepper flakes**, and **nutmeg**. Increase the heat to high and cook, stirring often, until all the liquid has evaporated and the vegetables are tender, 7 to 10 minutes. Add the **ground turkey** and cook, using a wooden spoon or spatula to break it up into tiny crumbles, until it's cooked through and no longer pink, 5 to 7 minutes.

3. Stir in the **diced tomatoes**, **tomato puree**, **salt**, and **half-and-half**. Grate the zest of the **lemon** directly into the pot. Bring to a simmer, then reduce the heat to medium-low and cook, uncovered, for 1½ to 2 hours, stirring twice an hour. It should only bubble every now and then—no rapid bubbling. The sauce is ready when it looks very thick, like sloppy joe meat. If, at the 2-hour mark, your sauce is still liquidy, crank up the heat to high and stir frequently until it thickens.

4. About 30 minutes before you're ready to eat, bring a large pot of salted water to a boil over high heat. Add the **pasta** and cook until al dente according to the package instructions. Scoop out **1 cup of the pasta cooking water**, then drain the pasta and add it to the pot of Bolognese along with ¼ cup of the reserved pasta cooking water and ¼ cup of the **Parm**. Cook over medium-low heat, stirring constantly, until the pasta is cooked to your liking and the sauce has thickened further and is sticking to the pasta, 3 to 4 minutes. Add another splash of pasta cooking water as needed to reach your desired consistency. Taste and adjust the flavors (more cheese and/or salt, **black pepper**!) as needed.

5. Divide the pasta among bowls and top with the remaining Parm.

MISO-MAPLE HAM

with Collard Greens

1 (6- to 8-pound) fully cooked
   bone-in unsliced smoked
   ham
¾ cup white miso paste
¾ cup maple syrup
3 bunches collard greens
   (about 3 pounds)
1 large yellow onion
¼ cup apple cider vinegar, plus
   more as needed
¼ cup extra-virgin olive oil
1 teaspoon kosher salt, plus
   more as needed
½ teaspoon freshly ground
   black pepper, plus more as
   needed

SWAP
If you can only
find a spiral-cut smoked ham,
you can use it-bake the ham
for only 1 1/2 hours total,
adding all the glaze at the
beginning.

Any hearty green such as kale
or Swiss chard will work in
place of the collards.

SERVES 8 TO 10

I do not love traditional holiday fare—in my opinion, roasted turkey can take a hike. We've hosted my parents for Thanksgiving a couple of times in California, and every single time I've both shocked their traditional Southern sensibilities by not serving turkey, and then absolutely delighted them by serving ham instead. This is my favorite show-off-y winter meal, holiday or no holiday.

1. Preheat the oven to 325°F.

2. Let the **ham** sit at room temperature while you prep everything.

3. In a small bowl, whisk together the **miso** and **maple syrup** until combined. Stem the **collard greens**, then cut the leaves into 1-inch-thick strips. Thinly slice the **onion**. In a large roasting pan, toss together the collard greens, onion, ¼ cup of the miso-maple mixture, the **vinegar**, **olive oil**, **salt**, and **pepper**.

4. Pat the ham dry. Use a sharp knife to create a crosshatch pattern in the skin and fat, about ¼ inch deep, making sure not to cut through to the meat. Place the ham on top of the greens in the pan, flat side down. Brush about half the remaining miso-maple mixture all over the ham.

5. Pour **4 cups water** over the collards (they won't be fully submerged) and bake the ham, uncovered, for 1 hour. Brush the ham with the remaining miso-maple mixture and stir the collards. Bake the ham for 1½ to 2 hours more, rotating the pan halfway through, until a crust has formed, an instant-read thermometer inserted into the thickest part of the ham registers 135°F, and the greens are very tender. If the glaze begins to brown too much, cover the ham with foil.

6. Transfer the ham to a cutting board and let rest for 15 minutes before slicing. Stir the collard greens and taste and add more salt, pepper, and vinegar as needed. Slice the ham and serve with a heap of the collard greens.

REALLY GOOD BEEF STEW
with Garlicky Fried Croutons

FOR THE STEW
3 large carrots
1 large fennel bulb
1 large yellow onion
4 garlic cloves
1 cup dried French green lentils
10 cups low-sodium beef
    stock (from three 1-quart
    containers)
2 pounds beef stew meat
1 cup farro
2 dried bay leaves
1 to 2 tablespoons mild harissa
    (1 will just flavor it, 2 will give
    it a kick)
2 tablespoons tomato paste
¾ teaspoon ground cumin
1 lemon
1 (8-ounce) block Parmesan
    cheese
Kosher salt
1 teaspoon freshly ground
    black pepper
1 large bunch collards

FOR THE CROUTONS
4 thick or 6 thin slices of
    absolutely any kind of bread
    (the better the bread, the
    better the crouton)
Extra-virgin olive oil
Kosher salt
¼ teaspoon garlic powder

SLOW To make this in a
slow cooker, dump in all the
stew ingredients, cover, and
cook on low for 6 hours.

SERVES 6 TO 8

To call this dish a beef stew is to vastly undersell the absolute masterpiece that it is. It has *so much flavor.* From the beef to the Parm to the harissa to the lemon—there's a lot going on, and it all melds together during a long slow simmer that turns this soup into a pot of gold. Beef stew meat is one of my favorite ingredients to bargain shop for—you can often find it on sale in the meat aisle. It's basically all the scraps from butchering beef, cut into tiny cubes, perfect for making stew!

1. **Make the stew:** Give the **carrots**, **fennel**, and **onion** a very coarse chop, then add them to a food processor along with the **garlic**. Pulse until very, very finely chopped, 10 to 15 pulses. Alternatively, you can chop them by hand.

2. Transfer the veggies to a large stockpot. Add the **lentils**, **stock**, **beef**, **farro**, **bay leaves**, **harissa**, **tomato paste**, and **cumin**. Grate in the zest of the **lemon** directly into the pot; set the zested lemon aside. Slice off the rind of the **Parm** and throw the rind in the pot too (set the cheese aside for serving). Season with **salt** and the **pepper**. Bring to a boil over high heat, then reduce the heat to low, cover, and cook for 2 hours, stirring every 20 minutes or so, until the beef is tender. In the last 30 minutes of cooking, stem and roughly chop the **collards** and stir them in.

3. **Meanwhile, make the croutons:** Cut enough **bread** into ½-inch cubes to make 4 cups. Warm a **huge glug of olive oil** in a large skillet over medium-high heat. When it shimmers, add the bread and stir to coat in the oil. Add more oil as needed to coat well.

4. Spread the bread into an even layer. Sprinkle generously with **salt** and the **garlic powder**. Cook, undisturbed, until golden brown on the first side, 3 to 5 minutes. Stir and cook until golden brown all over, 3 to 4 minutes more. Remove from the heat and let cool in the skillet.

5. If an oily fat layer has risen to the top of the stew, skim it off with a large spoon. Fish out the Parm rind and bay leaves and discard. Halve the zested lemon and squeeze the juice into the pot, then stir.

6. Ladle the stew into bowls. Top with the garlicky croutons and so much **Parm** that it looks like it snowed on your bowl. Seriously, that part is very important. Enjoy!

BAKED TOMATO BASIL BUTTER PASTA

6 garlic cloves

2 pounds cherry tomatoes

1 tablespoon extra-virgin olive oil

1 teaspoon sugar

1½ teaspoons kosher salt, plus more as needed

¼ teaspoon red pepper flakes, plus more for serving

8 ounces pasta (any short noodle)

3 basil sprigs

8 tablespoons (1 stick) unsalted butter

½ cup freshly grated Parmesan cheese, plus more for serving

SWAP
You can use any tomatoes here, but if they are not bite-size, squeeze out their liquidy insides first, otherwise your pasta will be too watery. Instead of butter, try swapping in a 5-ounce container of Garlic & Fine Herb Boursin cheese.

SERVES 3 OR 4

My sister, Annie, is perhaps my most loyal recipe follower—she and her husband, Nick, cook my recipes almost every night of the week. I made them this pasta when I was visiting them in North Carolina once, and now it's on their weekly rotation.

1. Preheat the oven to 425°F.

2. Smash and peel the **garlic**. In a 9 x 13-inch baking dish, combine the garlic, **tomatoes**, **olive oil**, **sugar**, **1 teaspoon of the salt**, and the **red pepper flakes**. Cover with foil and bake for 45 minutes, until the tomatoes are collapsing.

3. Remove from the oven (but leave the oven on). Scatter the **pasta** and **2 basil sprigs** over the top of the dish in an even layer. Smoosh the pasta down into the tomatoes and pour **1¼ cups hot water** (as hot as your sink will go—doesn't need to be boiling) over the top. The pasta should be covered in water, so add a bit more if needed. Add the **butter** right in the center of the pan. Sprinkle the remaining **½ teaspoon salt** over top. Cover with foil again (TIGHTLY) and bake for 30 minutes more, until the water is mostly absorbed and the pasta is almost tender.

4. Remove from the oven and reduce the oven temperature to 350°F. Discard the foil and basil sprigs and stir in the **Parm**. Return to the oven, uncovered, and bake for 5 to 10 minutes more, until the sauce thickens and the pasta is tender.

5. Meanwhile, pluck the leaves off the remaining **basil sprig** and thinly slice them.

6. Stir in the sliced basil and keep stirring until everything combines into a delicious tomato sauce. Taste and add more salt as needed. Garnish with more Parm and red pepper flakes and serve immediately.

GRILLED PICKLE CHICKEN SANDWICHES

4 boneless, skinless chicken
thighs (about 2 pounds total)
1 jar bread-and-butter pickles,
with their brine
½ cup mayonnaise
½ teaspoon chili powder
½ teaspoon ground cumin
Pinch of cayenne pepper
Pinch of kosher salt
Neutral oil
4 potato hamburger buns
4 slices provolone cheese
1 (8-ounce) bag shredded
iceberg lettuce
A big bag of plain potato chips
(I like Ruffles)

TIP
No grill? Place the chicken on a baking sheet and roast at 425°F for 15 to 20 minutes.

LEARN
Oiling the grill grates instead of the chicken will reduce oil dripping down into the flames, which could otherwise cause flare-ups.

RIFF
Thin out the sauce with a little bit of lemon juice to make a simple salad dressing. Toss with some iceberg and any chopped random veggies you have lying around and there ya go, salad!

SWAP
This marinade is excellent with any kind of chicken or pork chops.

SERVES 4

Every time I get to the bottom of a jar of bread and butter pickles (which, I should say, is often—my kids and I both inhale them), I rejoice: It's pickle chicken time. The sugar in the jarred brine helps tenderize the meat and helps it get beautifully brown on the grill. The size of the pickle jar literally does not matter for this recipe—use whatever jar you finish! I love serving these at a cookout where I might otherwise serve burgers. People's minds are blown when they taste these sweet and tangy grilled chicken sandos, and they're actually even easier to cook than burgers.

1. Place the **chicken** in a resealable plastic bag or large bowl. Add enough **pickle brine** to cover the chicken (about 1 cup; if you don't have quite enough to cover, give the chicken a stir after a few hours). Let marinate in the refrigerator for at least 12 hours and up to 24 hours.

2. Meanwhile, in a medium bowl, stir together the **mayonnaise**, **1 tablespoon pickle brine**, the **chili powder**, **cumin**, **cayenne**, and **salt**.

3. Heat an outdoor grill to medium-high (400° to 450°F).

4. Wad up a paper towel and soak it in **oil**. It should be saturated but not dripping. Grab the paper towel with heat-proof tongs and rub it all over the grill grates.

5. Open the **buns** and grill them cut side down with the lid open until lightly toasted, 1 to 2 minutes. Transfer to a serving platter and smear with chili mayo.

6. Remove the chicken thighs from the brine, letting any excess drop off and shaking them as dry as you can. Add the chicken to the direct heat side of the grill and cook for 5 to 6 minutes, or until grill marks appear on the bottom and it releases easily from the grill. Flip the chicken, add **1 slice of cheese** on top, and cook until the cheese is melted and an instant-read thermometer inserted into the chicken registers 165°F, about 5 minutes more.

7. Transfer the chicken to a plate and let it rest and cool for a few minutes.

8. Pile the grilled chicken, tons of **pickles**, and a handful of **iceberg** onto the toasted buns. Enjoy immediately with **potato chips** alongside and the extra chili mayo for dipping it all.

ROASTED PEANUT CARROT SOUP

2 pounds carrots
1 large red onion
2 medium Pink Lady or
   Honeycrisp apples
¼ cup extra-virgin olive oil
Kosher salt and freshly ground
   black pepper
4 to 6 cups low-sodium
   vegetable stock
1½ cups roasted salted peanuts
1 tablespoon apple cider
   vinegar, plus more as needed
½ teaspoon ground ginger, plus
   more as needed
⅛ teaspoon cayenne pepper

RIFF
Use only 2 1/2 cups of stock to make a peanut-carrot puree that is excellent served under grilled chicken or steak, like mashed potatoes.

SWAP
Use 3/4 cup peanut butter in place of the peanuts in the soup. If there's a peanut allergy, use any nut or seed butter instead. Use any roasted crunchy nut or garlicky fried croutons (see page 230) for topping.

SERVES 8

The summer between when George got out of the Navy and started business school, we decided to do something totally new to us: We packed up the car and headed to Telluride, Colorado, for three months. I got a job as a prep cook at 221 South Oak Bistro, a charming fine-dining restaurant in the heart of town. One of the core menu items was the "soup flight"—a trio of seasonal soups—and I was often put in charge of cooking them. The peanut soup was a puree of seasonal veggies and, believe it or not, at one of the fanciest restaurants in town, Skippy peanut butter and it was *absolutely perfect*. I've riffed on it many times over the years, and this is my favorite version. You'll use peanuts instead of peanut butter so you can employ them later on as a crunchy topping, something that in my opinion, takes soup from good to great.

1. Preheat the oven to 375°F.

2. Wash the **carrots** (no need to peel or chop them). Chop the **onion** into 6 big pieces. Chop the **apples** into 4 big pieces each and core them. Throw everything on a baking sheet and toss with the **olive oil**, **2 teaspoons salt**, and **½ teaspoon black pepper**. Roast for 1 hour, or until the carrots are fork-tender.

3. Meanwhile, in a high-powered blender, combine **4 cups of the stock** and **1 cup of the peanuts** and let soak while the veggies roast.

4. Use tongs to transfer the roasted veggies to the blender, scraping in any roasty bits or oil that might be left on the baking sheet. Add the **vinegar**, **ginger**, and **cayenne**. Hold the lid on firmly with a kitchen towel (the blender will be very full, and the hot vegetables will create pressure and try to blow the lid off!) and blend, starting on low speed and gradually moving up to high speed, until completely smooth. Depending on the size of your veggies, and how thick you like your soups, you may need to add more stock to get a nice smooth consistency; blend it in a splash at a time until it's perfect.

5. Taste and add more salt, vinegar, or ginger as desired. Chop the remaining **½ cup peanuts** into very small pieces. Serve the soup with the chopped peanuts on top.

BO SSAM

FOR THE PORK
1 (6- to 8-pound) bone-in pork butt
4 tablespoons plus 1 teaspoon brown sugar
2 tablespoons kosher salt
2 teaspoons freshly ground black pepper

FOR THE GINGER-SCALLION SAUCE
6 scallions
¼ cup pickled ginger
⅓ cup sesame oil
⅓ cup rice vinegar (or any light-colored vinegar)
1 tablespoon soy sauce
1 teaspoon brown sugar

FOR SERVING
2 cups sushi rice, rinsed
1 head butter lettuce
Toppings (optional): chopped peanuts, shredded carrots, chopped cucumbers, chopped cilantro

SERVES 8 TO 10

Every December, we rent a house somewhere cool in Northern California with our friends the Huffards and the Georges for an annual "Sexy Santa" weekend. Like most inside jokes, the reason we call it Sexy Santa is totally dumb: One of our husbands jokingly suggested our secret Santa gift exchange should be "sexy" the first year we did it, and the name just stuck. We gather our hordes of children (eight little boys and one little girl!) for a weekend of eating, drinking, gift exchanging, wrestling, and general holiday merriment. On the Saturday evening, we dress up in our finest and sit down for a fancy grown-up dinner after the kids have gone to bed. For four years running, we've made bo ssam—slow-roasted pork butt with rice, lettuce wraps, tons of crunchy toppings, and delicious sauces. If you've never roasted a pork butt (aka pork shoulder) before, prepare to be legitimately shocked by what an incredible cook you are. The ease of transforming a massive cut of cheap meat into the most tender, juicy, flavorful meat you've ever had is honestly a bit mind-blowing the first time you do it. When people tell me they need something really easy to serve a crowd, bo ssam is always my answer.

1. **Make the pork:** Position a rack in the center of the oven and preheat to 275°F. Line a rimmed baking sheet with aluminum foil.

2. Place the **pork butt** on the prepared baking sheet and pat dry with paper towels. Rub the **brown sugar**, **salt**, and **pepper** all over it, including into any grooves. Roast, fat side up, until the pork shreds easily and an instant-read thermometer inserted into the pork registers 195°F. This will take anywhere from 4 to 8 hours, depending on the size of your butt and the size of your oven. After 4 hours, check the internal temperature every 30 minutes to avoid overcooking (but also don't stress—it's hard to screw this one up).

3. **Make the ginger-scallion sauce:** Soon after putting the pork in the oven, or up to 48 hours before you're ready to eat, thinly slice the **scallions**. Mince the **pickled ginger**. Combine the scallions and ginger in a bowl with the **sesame oil**, **vinegar**, **soy sauce**, and **brown sugar**.

4. Ten minutes before removing the pork from the oven, start the rice: In a medium saucepan, combine the **rice** and **2⅓ cups water** and bring to a boil over high heat. Reduce the heat to low, cover, and cook for 15 to 17 minutes, until the liquid is absorbed and the rice is tender. Turn off the heat and let the rice steam, still covered, for about 10 minutes more.

5. Remove the pork and let it rest until it's cool enough to handle, 15 to 20 minutes. While it's resting, carefully pull the leaves of the **butter lettuce** apart and wash and dry them. Place on a serving platter along with the sauce and any toppings. Use two forks to shred the meat, mixing the crispy outside layer with the inner juicy bits. Discard the bone and any big hunks of fat.

6. Allow people to build their own lettuce wraps, rice bowls, or lettuce and rice bowls! It's a do-your-thing kind of meal.

RATATOUILLE LASAGNA

1 large (1½- to 2-pound) globe
   eggplant
1 large (8-ounce) zucchini
1 large (6-ounce) yellow squash
1 small yellow onion
4 garlic cloves
⅓ cup extra-virgin olive oil, plus
   more as needed
Kosher salt
½ teaspoon red pepper flakes
2 teaspoons dried Italian
   seasoning, plus more as
   needed
2 (28-ounce) cans diced
   tomatoes
1 (8-ounce) container
   mascarpone cheese
1 cup packed fresh basil leaves
1 (9-ounce) package no-boil
   lasagna noodles
8 ounces shredded mozzarella
   cheese

SERVES 6

I've posted several one-pot pasta recipes on Instagram that have gone *viral*. If you've ever had a video go viral on the internet, you know that this is a truly wild time, wherein both the loveliest of compliments and the most egregious of insults are hurled with abandon on your proverbial internet doorstep. The "true Italians" of the internet think that a one-skillet lasagna, wherein we made a sauce and then smoosh no-boil noodles straight down into it, no layering necessary, is an actual blight upon humanity. I, conversely, think it's an absolutely delightful way to get a homemade lasagna onto the dinner table without dirtying every dish in your kitchen.

1. Preheat the oven to 375°F.

2. Peel and cut the **eggplant**, **zucchini**, and **squash** into ½-inch pieces. Dice the **onion** and mince the **garlic**.

3. Warm the **olive oil** in a Dutch oven or an ovenproof skillet with high sides over medium-high heat. Add the eggplant, zucchini, squash, onion, and **1½ teaspoons salt** and cook, stirring occasionally, until they are just beginning to get tender, 4 to 5 minutes. Stir in the garlic, **red pepper flakes**, and **Italian seasoning** and cook for 2 minutes more.

4. Stir in the **tomatoes**, half the **mascarpone**, and **1½ teaspoons salt**. Bring it to a boil over high heat. Simmer over medium-low heat for 30 minutes. Turn it down to low if it starts to bubble aggressively. Meanwhile, thinly slice the **basil** and stir almost all of it into the pot (save some for garnish).

5. Turn off the stove. Taste and season with more salt or Italian seasoning as needed. Push the **noodles** into the pot, doing your best to layer in the sauce, like a lasagna. Break noodles in half to fill the edges as needed—but nothing about this is a perfect science. Just shove those noodles in there! Make sure that the top layer of noodles is covered in sauce. Dollop the remaining **mascarpone** on top, then sprinkle with the **mozzarella**.

6. Bake for 30 minutes. Let the baked lasagna sit for at least 10 minutes before slicing and serving. Top with the reserved basil and enjoy.

RIFF
Make ratatouille pasta! Add only one can of diced tomatoes, then simmer the sauce for 15 minutes. Stir in 1 pound of cooked pasta and crumble a bit of goat cheese on top of everyone's bowl.

SHORTCUT
Skip the 30-minute simmer by using two 28-ounce jars of a tomato-basil pasta sauce instead of the canned tomatoes. Omit the Italian seasoning and 1 1/2 teaspoons salt. Stir the sauce into the veggies, add your noodles, and bake.

BULK IT UP
Sauté 1 pound sausage (casings removed) in the pot first, breaking it into small pieces, then continue the recipe as written, adding the oil and veggies into the pot with the cooked sausage.

PIZZA INSALATA

3 tablespoons extra-virgin olive oil
1 pound store-bought fresh pizza dough
4 garlic cloves
2 cups (8 ounces) shredded mozzarella cheese
2 ounces goat cheese
2 ounces grated Asiago cheese
1½ cups packed arugula
1 tablespoon balsamic vinegar
Kosher salt

TIP Check the freezer aisle for balls of fresh pizza dough. If you can't find it there or in the refrigerated section, many local pizza shops will sell you some of their fresh dough.

RIFF Store-bought pesto or pizza sauce would both be delicious instead of the oil and garlic base. Or, use this method to make literally any pizza. Pepperoni with hot honey! Mushroom! Bacon and pineapple!

BULK IT UP To add meat, try adding cooked sausage or pepperoni to the pizza, or shredded rotisserie chicken to the salad.

SERVES 4 TO 6

I went to boarding school thousands of miles from home, at the Lawrenceville School in New Jersey. One of my best friends, Nellie, was a day student, and her family adopted me into their home, showed up at my sports games, and even let me move in for several months my junior year. Every Sunday night, the entire family would get the biggest table at Teresa's, a pizza spot in the heart of Princeton. Anyone was invited—from teenagers to Nellie's grandparents and their friends. I can still feel the warmth of those meals, and I can still taste my order: pizza insalata. It was a simple cheese pizza with a vinegary salad piled on top, the most perfect juxtaposition of flavors and textures. I almost never see pizza insalata on menus, so I came up with my own version many years ago, and it's one of my favorite meals when I want something carby and cheesy, but I also need a heap of vegetables.

1. Coat a 12-inch cast-iron skillet with **2 tablespoons of the olive oil**. Plop the **pizza dough** right down in the center of the pan and flip it around to coat it in oil. Cover the ball tightly with plastic wrap and leave it at room temperature for at least 30 minutes or up to 2 hours (the longer it sits, the better).

2. Position a rack in the lower third of the oven and preheat to 475°F (or the hottest it will go).

3. When the dough has been out for (at least) 30 minutes, uncover it and discard the plastic wrap. Return it to the skillet and use your fingers to "dimple" the pizza dough out until it fills the entire skillet. Use a Microplane to grate the **garlic** all over the crust. Use your fingers to spread it around evenly.

4. Sprinkle the **mozzarella**, **goat cheese**, and **Asiago** all the way to the edges of the skillet.

5. Bake the pizza for 17 to 20 minutes, until the underside of the crust is golden brown (use a spatula to lift it up and take a peek). If the bottom looks good but the top needs more time, transfer the pizza to the top rack of the oven for a few minutes to get brown on top.

6. Remove the pizza from the oven and place it on the stovetop to cool. Run a spatula around the edges of the pizza to detach it from the skillet. Let it cool for a few minutes, then use a spatula to slide it onto a cutting board.

7. While it's cooling, combine the **arugula**, **balsamic**, remaining **1 tablespoon olive oil**, and a **big pinch of salt** in a large bowl. Toss gently until evenly coated.

8. Sprinkle the salad over the pizza, cut, and devour immediately.

OBLIGATORY GREENS

SAUTÉED GREENS

Heat **3 tablespoons extra-virgin olive oil** in your largest skillet over medium heat. When it shimmers, add **2 to 4 thinly sliced garlic cloves** and cook, stirring, until fragrant, about 30 seconds. Add **1 bunch coarsely chopped tough cooking greens** (such as collards, Swiss chard, stemmed kale, or escarole) and **⅓ cup stock or water**, and use tongs to smoosh the greens down into the stock as much as possible. Cover and cook for 5 to 7 minutes, until the greens are very tender.

Uncover and cook, stirring frequently, until all the liquid has evaporated, 1 to 2 minutes more. Season however you like—but at a minimum, **lots of salt** and **a little pepper**. Stir in **1 to 2 tablespoons of any vinegar** before serving.

THE GREATEST KALE SALAD

In a large bowl, combine **½ cup freshly grated Parmesan**, **¼ cup extra-virgin olive oil**, the zest and juice of **1 lemon**, **1 grated garlic clove**, and a **pinch of red pepper flakes**. Whisk to mix well. This will *not* look like your average salad dressing. It'll be really thick and chunky.

Add **2 large bunches thinly sliced lacinato kale leaves** and sprinkle with **salt**. Using your hands, massage (aka squeeze) the kale about 7 times, tossing it with the salad dressing, until tender. Taste and add more **salt** as needed.

RIFF

Add chicken nuggets (yes, the ones from the freezer section) for a crispy chicken salad.

In the summer, add thinly sliced nectarines and almonds and serve with any grilled meat or fish.

Add 2 cups shredded rotisserie chicken and wrap in a tortilla or lavash bread for a chicken Caesar-ish wrap.

WELL-DRESSED TENDER GREENS

Pile as much **arugula**, **spinach**, or **mixed greens** as you need for your group into a large bowl. Use your left hand to toss the greens as you use your right hand to drizzle **extra-virgin olive oil** over the top, stopping as soon as they're lightly coated. Continue tossing in this manner while you add a drizzle of **really good balsamic vinegar** and a **sprinkle each of salt and pepper**. Use a vegetable peeler to shave **ribbons of Parmesan** directly into the salad.

RIFF

Add quinoa, yellow raisins, and chopped toasted almonds.

Add thinly sliced roasted red peppers, white beans, and cubed cheddar.

Add chopped cooked beets, blue cheese, and toasted hazelnuts.

CRISP GREENS
with Lemon Vinaigrette

In a large serving bowl, whisk together the zest and juice of **1 lemon**, **1 tablespoon clear vinegar** (such as red wine, apple cider, or champagne), **3 tablespoons extra-virgin olive oil**, and **1 teaspoon kosher salt**. Add **3 cups roughly chopped crisp greens** such as butter lettuce, romaine, or Little Gem and toss to coat well.

RIFF

Add strawberries, goat cheese, and candied walnuts.

Add pickled onion, grilled corn, Cotija cheese, and roasted red pepper.

Add peaches, feta, toasted almonds, and fresh dill.

OBLIGATORY SWEETS

CARAMELIZED PEACH SNICKERDOODLE COBBLER

6 medium peaches, thinly sliced, or 2 (10-ounce) bags frozen peaches

⅔ cup packed brown sugar

3 tablespoons cornstarch

2 teaspoons pure vanilla extract

1½ teaspoons ground cinnamon

1 cup all-purpose flour

1½ teaspoons baking powder

¾ teaspoon kosher salt

½ cup (1 stick) unsalted butter, melted

½ cup buttermilk

1 tablespoon granulated sugar

1 pint vanilla ice cream, for serving (optional)

SWAP

You can use 2 pounds of basically any fruit here. Apple and blueberry would be especially delicious with the snickerdoodle topping!

SERVES 6

My mom is one of five siblings, and each of those siblings had three or four kids, and each of us kids have had two or three of our own kids . . . so there are a lot of us Thompson cousins. Every July, we descend upon Bald Head Island, North Carolina, for a week of beach games, shrimp eating, and beer drinking. Without fail, every single carful of cousins stops at one of the many peach stands along the final stretch of road before the ferry dock and grabs a massive basket of peaches. We proceed to spend days talking about what we should do with the hundreds of peaches sitting on the counter at every single house. This snickerdoodle cobbler was born out of just such a peach surplus and, in my opinion, is hands down the most fabulous way to consume a peach.

1. Preheat the oven to 375°F.

2. In a 10-inch pie dish or ovenproof dish of any kind, combine the **peaches**, **⅓ cup of the brown sugar**, the **cornstarch**, **vanilla**, and **½ teaspoon of the cinnamon**. Toss to combine and coat the peaches evenly.

3. In a large bowl, combine the **flour**, remaining **⅓ cup brown sugar**, **½ teaspoon of the cinnamon**, and **½ teaspoon of the salt**. Stir in the **melted butter** and **buttermilk**. Whisk until smooth.

4. Use a spatula to scrape the batter from the bowl on top of the peaches, covering them. Bake for 30 to 40 minutes, until the topping is browned and the juices are bubbling around the edges of the pan.

5. In a small bowl, stir together the remaining **½ teaspoon cinnamon**, the **granulated sugar**, and the remaining **¼ teaspoon salt**.

6. Remove the cobbler from the oven and immediately sprinkle the cinnamon-sugar on top. Let rest for 5 minutes, then scoop into bowls. Serve topped with ice cream, if desired.

PEANUT BUTTER CUP POTS DE CRÈME

1½ cups (8 ounces) semisweet
   or dark chocolate chips
2 tablespoons peanut butter
3 large eggs, at room
   temperature
2 teaspoons pure vanilla
   extract
Pinch of kosher salt
⅔ cup milk of your choice
   (I love using oat milk)
1 tablespoon sugar (optional)
5 ounces store-bought
   whipped cream

LEARN Don't stress about
the raw eggs here—blending
them with the hot liquid makes
them safe for consumption!

If you want to use milk
chocolate, reduce the amount
of milk to 1/3 cup. Milk
chocolate actually has . . .
milk in it! The mixture will
be too liquidy unless you
reduce the milk.

RIFF Make a mint chocolate
pot de crème by omitting the
peanut butter and adding 1/2
teaspoon peppermint extract.
Sprinkle crushed candy canes
on top.

SERVES 6

What to cook when you don't feel like making dessert? These little pots of
delicious pudding. They require less than 10 minutes of initial effort—after that,
they just hang out in the fridge for a few hours until it's time to eat. Your diners
will think you whisked chocolate over a double boiler for hours, when really you
just gave a bunch of deliciousness a quick whirl in the blender.

1. In a blender, combine the **chocolate**, **peanut butter**, **eggs**, **vanilla**, and **salt**.
   Blend on high speed until coarsely combined, about 30 seconds.

2. Microwave the **milk** in a microwave-safe mug or bowl in 20-second
   intervals until very, very hot to the touch. Pour the hot milk into the
   blender with the chocolate mixture and blend until smooth.

3. Taste. Do you want it to be sweeter? If so, blend in up to **1 tablespoon
   sugar**.

4. Pour the mixture into six small bowls/ramekins/teacups and refrigerate
   for at least 1 hour for a pudding-y consistency or up to 4 hours for a more
   firm ganache-y consistency.

5. Serve with a dollop of **whipped cream**.

SALTED BROWN BUTTER TOFFEE SKILLET COOKIE

1 cup (2 sticks) unsalted butter
1 (2-ounce) dark chocolate bar
2 (1.4-ounce) chocolate-toffee
   candy bars (such as Skor)
1 cup lightly packed dark brown
   sugar
⅓ cup granulated sugar
1 large egg
1 large egg yolk
1 tablespoon pure vanilla
   extract
2 cups all-purpose flour
1 teaspoon baking soda
½ teaspoon kosher salt
1½ teaspoons flaky sea salt
Vanilla ice cream, for serving
   (optional, but highly
   recommended)

RIFF

To make this dough into individual cookies, scoop 2-tablespoon balls of dough onto a parchment-lined baking sheet and bake at 375°F for 8 to 10 minutes, until golden brown on the outside but still light golden brown in the center.

To make more perfectly square pieces, transfer the dough to an 8-inch square baking dish, then bake for 25 to 30 minutes, until light golden on top.

SWAP

In place of the toffee, swap in M&M's or just a handful of chocolate chips; add 2 tablespoons espresso powder for even richer flavor. Or omit the chocolate chips and toffee and swap in 1 1/2 cups of rainbow sprinkles for a brown butter birthday cake cookie. Rise & Roam bakery in Carmel has a life-changing toffee potato chip cookie, so I also recommend throwing in a handful of salted potato chips.

MAKES ONE 10- OR 12-INCH SKILLET COOKIE

Our friends Cheetah and Frank live in San Francisco but come down to Carmel Valley to visit us regularly with their son, Hamer (my godson!). We live in a pretty tiny house, so they typically stay at a hotel nearby, but one time, we all wanted to be able to put the kids to sleep and hang out and not have to deal with babysitters, so they decided to camp out in our yard! It was the most fun, ridiculous weekend. I filled them up with lots of beautiful food and fabulous wine to thank them for sleeping on the ground in order to hang out with me. One night, knowing all about Frank's sweet tooth, I served this over-the-top skillet cookie—and they went absolutely insane. Since then, it's become my party trick—a few hours after dinner, when everyone's getting a bit peckish again, I emerge from the kitchen with this gigantic cookie goodness, topped with several scoops of ice cream. The crowd goes wild.

1. Preheat the oven to 325°F.

2. Melt the **butter** in a 10- to 12-inch ovenproof skillet over medium heat, swirling the skillet often, until the butter foams, then cook until the milk solids drop to the bottom and begin to brown, 5 to 8 minutes total. If the melted butter starts to bubble and pop out of the skillet, reduce the heat to medium-low. Remove the skillet from the heat and let cool in the refrigerator for 10 minutes.

3. Meanwhile, chop the **chocolate bar** and **chocolate-toffee bars** into small pieces.

4. Add the **brown sugar** and **granulated sugar** to the skillet with the cooled butter and stir to combine. Stir in the **egg**, **egg yolk**, and **vanilla**.

5. Pile the **flour**, **baking soda**, and **salt** on top of the butter mixture. Use your fingers to sift the baking soda into the flour, then stir it into the butter mixture. (It will seem like too much flour at first, but just keep stirring until combined.)

6. Stir the chopped chocolate and toffee into the dough; you might have to use your hands to incorporate them well. Press the dough to the edges of the skillet and smooth out the top. Sprinkle with the **flaky salt**.

7. If you can stand to wait, let the dough rest at room temperature for at least 30 minutes to allow the flour to hydrate before baking. Bake for 20 to 30 minutes, until the cookie is light golden but still very soft-looking in the center. A 12-inch skillet will need less time; a 10-inch skillet will need a few minutes more.

8. Top with **ice cream**, if desired, and immediately dig in with spoons, or let the cookie cool completely (about 20 minutes), then cut into slices or squares before serving.

LEMON CAKE
with Crème Fraîche Frosting

FOR THE CAKE

½ cup (1 stick) unsalted butter
2 large lemons
1 cup granulated sugar
3 large eggs
1½ teaspoons pure vanilla extract
8 ounces crème fraîche, at room temperature
1½ cups all-purpose flour
1 teaspoon baking powder
¼ teaspoon baking soda
½ teaspoon kosher salt
1 (3.4-ounce) package lemon pudding mix (such as Jell-O)

FOR THE FROSTING

1 cup (2 sticks) unsalted butter, at room temperature
8 ounces crème fraîche, at room temperature
3 cups powdered sugar
1 tablespoon fresh lemon juice
1 teaspoon pure vanilla extract
Pinch of kosher salt

TIP Garnish the cake with more lemon zest, if you're feelin' fancy.

LEARN Save your butter wrappers! They're the perfect thing to use for greasing baking dishes—just rub the wrapper all over the dish.

RIFF Make cupcakes instead! Line a cupcake pan with paper liners and scoop batter into the liners to fill them three-quarters of the way. Bake for 20 to 25 minutes, until a toothpick inserted into the center of a cupcake comes out clean. Let them cool completely before frosting.

SERVES 9

This cake is an ode to my son Mattis, who shares my principles for desserts: No nuts are allowed in cookies or brownies; mint chocolate chip ice cream or bust; a good chocolate chip cookie over absolutely everything, but anything lemon is a close second. This extra moist lemon cake with tangy crème fraîche frosting is what Mattis and my dessert dreams are made of.

1. **Make the cake:** Preheat the oven to 350°F. Grease an 8-inch baking dish (see Riff).

2. Melt the **butter** in a small saucepan over medium heat. Remove from the heat and let cool.

3. Zest the **lemons** into a large bowl to get 2 tablespoons of zest. Add the **granulated sugar** and pinch the zest and sugar together until combined. Whisk in the **eggs** aggressively for 2 minutes; your wrists will be tired, but this will help make the cake fluffy.

4. Whisk in the melted butter and **vanilla**, then add the **crème fraîche** and stir until everything is combined.

5. Add the **flour** in a pile right on top of the wet ingredients, but do not mix yet. Add the **baking powder**, **baking soda**, **salt**, and **lemon pudding mix** on top of the flour and use your fingers to sift it all together. Stir just to combine; do not overmix. Pour the mixture into the prepared baking dish and smooth out the top.

6. Bake for 40 to 50 minutes, until the top of the cake is golden and feels firm to the touch and a tester inserted into the center comes out clean. Remove from the oven and let the cake cool completely, about 20 minutes.

7. **Meanwhile, make the frosting:** In a large bowl, stir the **butter** with a rubber spatula to get it as soft as possible. Do your best to get it really smooth, then stir in the **crème fraîche**, incorporating it a little bit at a time. Add the **powdered sugar** 1 cup at a time, using a fork to sift it and get out any lumps. This is very important! Now stir it all together, using a spatula to forcefully smooth out any lumps. Stir in the **lemon juice**, **vanilla**, and **salt**.

8. Slather the cooled cake with the frosting. Slice into 9 squares and serve.

Recipes by Protein

BEEF, LAMB & PORK

VEGETARIAN & EGGS

What to Cook When . . .

YOU WANT TO SHOW OFF

YOU WANT TO USE YOUR SLOW COOKER

Acknowledgments

To **George**, my Jeffrey: Your palate is still as undiscerning as the day we met, but I can't complain about the fact that your default recipe feedback is "this is the best thing you've ever cooked." My ego appreciates it, even if your tasting notes are lackluster. I adore you and our feral children.

To my beasts, **Mattis**, **Calum**, and **Cashel**: Someday I'll tell you all about how I wrote this book in between school pickups, swim lessons, nap time, potty training, scooter rides, tide pool walks, meltdowns, dancing to Taylor Swift and Billy Joel in the kitchen, giggle attacks, diaper changes, and living out of multiple rental homes while our house was renovated. But for now, I'll just continue to soak up every minute of the chaos. You are my dream guys.

To my team at Union Square—**Lisa Forde**, **Renée Bollier**, **Caroline Hughes**, **Ivy McFadden**, and **Kevin Iwano**—and to **Ian Dingman**: Wow, you guys, this book! Look how beautiful it is! You did that. Thank you.

To my editor, **Amanda Englander**: thank you for hunting me down and making me write this book. Working with you on it has been pure joy. You are so good at what you do. And of course, thank you to Amanda's bestie group chat for weighing in on . . . everything.

To my agent, **Sarah Smith**, who went on maternity leave only a month after I came back from maternity leave, and managed to sell this book during that brief window where neither of us had a brand-new baby. Women rule. You rule. Love you.

To **Ali Slagle**, who tested and gave such insightful feedback on every single recipe in this book. You made *What to Cook* a better book, and I'm so grateful to have worked with you.

To **my parents**, for making me believe that I can do anything.

To my sister, **Annie**: This cookbook was fueled by our shared audiobook accounts. Don't be surprised if you find an X-rated typo on an ingredient list somewhere.

To **Amy** and **Gray**, my September triplet baby mamas, for helping me keep my head on straight while I birthed a baby boy and a book baby in the same nine-month period. Thank you for heaping praise on me when you knew I needed a boost, and for meeting me halfway when I needed a hug.

To **Cheetah**, for knowing when I need tough love and when I need ice cream cake.

To **Tannia**, **Quinn**, and **Gema**, the wonderful women who are helping me raise kind boys.

To all of my **mom friends** (you know who you are!), who are constantly telling me that I'm doing a *GREAT JOB* even when I'm quite sure that I'm doing a mediocre job.

To **Molly Ramsey**, who has been writing, editing, recipe testing, and a million other things to make *What to Cook* the newsletter the success that it is since the very start—I couldn't have done this without you and I am so grateful you're on my team.

To the **cousin blog**, my biggest cheerleaders: I won the genetic lottery with you.

To the longtime *What to Cook* subscribers and loyal @carochambers girls who have cheered me on and supported me for years and years: This book is for you.

Index

UNION
SQUARE
& CO.
NEW YORK

ISBN 978-1-4549-5271-8
ISBN 978-1-4549-5272-5 (e-book)

For information about custom editions, special
sales, and premium purchases, please contact
specialsales@unionsquareandco.com.

Printed in the United States of America

2 4 6 8 10 9 7 5 3

unionsquareandco.com

Editor: Amanda Englander
Designer: Ian Dingman
Photographer: Eva Kolenko
Prop Stylist: Genesis Vallejo
Food Stylists: Lillian Kang and Paige Arnett
Art Director: Renée Bollier
Project Editor: Ivy McFadden
Production Manager: Kevin Iwano
Copy Editor: Terry Deal